How to be a Successful Indie Writer

Dale T. Phillips

Thanks for being a reader.

Dale

Dale T. Phillips

Try these other works by Dale T. Phillips

Shadow of the Wendigo (Supernatural Thriller)
Neptune City (Mystery)

The Zack Taylor Mystery Series
A Darkened Room
A Sharp Medicine
A Certain Slant of Light
A Shadow on the Wall
A Fall From Grace
A Memory of Grief

Story Collections
The Big Book of Genre Stories (Different Genres)
Halls of Horror (Horror)
Deadly Encounters (3 Zack Taylor Mystery/Crime Tales)
The Return of Fear (Scary Stories)
Five Fingers of Fear (Scary Stories)
Jumble Sale (Different Genres)
Crooked Paths (Mystery/Crime)
More Crooked Paths (Mystery/Crime)
The Last Crooked Paths (Mystery/Crime)
Fables and Fantasies (Fantasy)
More Fables and Fantasies (Fantasy)
Strange Tales (Magic Realism, Paranormal)
Apocalypse Tango (End of the World)

Non-fiction Career Help
How to be a Successful Indie Writer
How to Improve Your Interviewing Skills

Dale T. Phillips

With Other Authors
Rogue Wave: Best New England Crime Stories 2015
Red Dawn: Best New England Crime Stories 2016
Windward: Best New England Crime Stories 2017

Sign up for my newsletter to get special offers
http://www.daletphillips.com

Contents

How to Be a Successful Indie Writer

Foreword

As this is written, we live in an insane time, with the world gripped by a plague, and many of us at great risk. We are all vulnerable, and any piece of writing might be our last. Writing is a revolutionary act, creating is hard, especially with the threat of annihilation so close. So make your writing count. Tell the tales that must be told, say the things that are true, pour yourself and all you are into your work. Communicate your inner vision to the outside world. You may be unsure of yourself, especially since what you fear and what you want are the same thing, but it's a worthwhile journey. There's no feeling like seeing your book for sale in a bookstore window, or someone on the subway reading a copy of something you've written.

The old world of Big Publishing/Traditional Publishing may not survive the changes being wrought. The big business of publishing books has been tap-dancing on the edge of the abyss for years. They rely on huge profits, accurate future forecasts, a great deal of luck, and a distribution model that is outdated, because the world has changed completely. Darwin said the species that survive are the most *adaptable*, and Big Publishing (currently at a handful of multinational corporations, mostly foreign-owned) does not adapt quickly, or well.

This is not bad news for Independent (Indie) writers, who have agility and the ability to adapt quickly. As a business, our costs can be small, we can change direction rapidly, and our profits have no upper limits. We have so few limitations or restrictions on what we can do, with a world of possibility.

This book focuses on success for the fiction writer, even though many of the techniques and ideas can be applied to other types. Other book types have their own issues and success methods, and publication and formatting can be vastly different.

I'm constantly getting more and more requests to inform or assist people in learning about the writing and publishing processes. This book is not the be-all and end-all, but a useful atlas for the parameters of your journey, showing you how the pieces fit together in relation to each other. It tells you what to expect, gives tips on things you'll need on the journey, helpful pointers to stay on the path, and good examples to follow. Since no one book can contain everything to know, along the way you'll want other, more specific guidebooks that focus on each particular feature.

There will be occasional bits of repetition, as some areas are important not to miss, and crop up in multiple topics. May this book have value for you, to make you aware of the possibilities and the rewards for being an Indie writer. You have a good chance of achieving success by planning and working toward it, and this book is a guide and a pointer to many other resources. Best of luck in your journey.

***

Dale T. Phillips

Introduction

"Far better is it to dare mighty things, win glorious triumphs, even checkered by failures, than to take rank with those poor spirits who neither enjoy much nor suffer much, because they live in the gray twilight which knows not victory or defeat."

—Theodore Roosevelt

Who am I to give advice on being a successful Indie writer? You haven't seen my name on the *NY Times* best-seller list, nor do I live on a yacht from my writing income. Well, many success books are written with techniques that worked only *for the author*, which may not necessarily be right for you. This book is from more than just my personal experiences, and distills the knowledge and success methods of dozens of successful writers, both Independent (Indie) and Traditional, with techniques and tips gleaned from books, articles, websites, blogs, conferences, personal accounts, and solid examples. There are a lot of helpful hints to help you choose your own path. Use what is useful to you, and disregard the rest, because there's a lot of contradictory advice out there. Some insist that there's only one right path (theirs), and that's nonsense.

Knowing a piece of information can save you time, money, and frustration. Much good information is here, which took a lot of time to gather, and which should save you hundreds of hours of having to dig it up and learn everything the hard way. There are entire books written on many of the topics here, so this is just the start of your research. No one book could cover everything, because by the time the book was finished (even with a team of writers), the information would be outdated, the book would be more than a thousand pages, and cost more than anyone would want to pay. This way, you likely will spend less time to learn much of what you need to know.

Many times, rather than including an exhaustive section that still wouldn't be complete, I refer to the Resources. It will take time to research them, but that's the process. In the online booksellers (or sometimes the library), or the website of the author, there will be a good explanation of each particular book on a topic. Look for information on the subject you want, and find what you need. Links get outdated over time, so when that occurs here, just use an online search engine on the Internet to find updated sources.

Credentials

For over thirty years, I've made my living as a professional writer— specifically Software Technical

How to Be a Successful Indie Writer

Writing for High-tech companies. Because of writing skills, I was able to provide a decent living for a family, even in times of bad economies. As in fiction writing, a Technical Writer has to be aware of audience, customer expectations, working with editors and feedback, deadlines, accuracy, and formatting. One has to know desktop publishing tools, how to be concise and thorough in the written word, transmit ideas into readable text, and figure out how to deliver the content in different formats. So all that gave me a leg up in becoming a successful Indie fiction writer.

I've been paid for a lot of different types of writing: fiction and non-fiction, technical book reviews, creating website content, career advice, gaming manual production, poetry, and more. In less than ten years I've published a string of good novels, a lot of stories, story collections, and non-fiction. Most of the fiction writing I create now gets sold in some fashion. Professional authors have praised my writing, and added their names as recommendations for my work. I give talks and workshops on aspects of writing and publishing, I've taught classes and seminars, and have appeared on television, radio, podcasts, and blogs to talk about all that. I've been on a number of panels at national conferences to share ideas, experiences, and information about writing and publishing. Every year gets busier, with more opportunities than I can deal with.

I've studied how to be a successful writer for a long time, from the dark old days of typewriters and return postage, to the new world of e-submissions. I've seen the changes in the publishing world first-hand, paying attention as a new paradigm was born. It's wonderful, and *the best time ever to be a writer*. For the first time in history, you have control, and you can do what you want, without having to wait for approval or permission from anybody else. This book is how you can become a success, following what many others did, and continue do. There are different paths, and we'll be pointing to some of them as potential guides for you as a starting place. The best part? It's okay to make mistakes. It's how we learn and grow. No career move is fatal, unlike so much of the Traditional path of the past.

Caveat

If your measure of success is merely sales, you'll want to spend time with the Resources Appendix, which has links to books and sites that tell you how to improve your sales numbers. My books sell in the thousands, not the hundreds of thousands, because I don't do all the marketing techniques that sell more. If I did all that, I could certainly sell more books, but my time is limited, and I didn't take up writing to become a professional *marketer*. Spending so much time chasing numbers wouldn't make me happy, and too many writers are obsessed about sales, when they should be focusing more on improving their craft and output.

How to Be a Successful Indie Writer

The real success recipe given here is pretty simple: *follow the path that makes you happy.* I'm one of the happiest writers around, as most others seem to be constantly complaining about something: agents, publishers, sales, awards, writer's block, etc. So I offer this book up as advice to someone who'd like to do well in a writing career. This is only the beginning of the sources of information you'll be checking out. The more you discover, the more you'll see much of the same good advice being repeated over and over. Most people would rather complain about what's wrong in their lives rather than do something about it, so take the steps on the path you want.

Waiting for other people to make your dreams come true is like waiting for a bus on a corner where there's no bus stop. Sometimes the bus driver may feel bad for you and stop anyways, but usually he'll speed right past and leave you standing there like an idiot.

—Kevin Hart, *I Can't Make This Up*

The book discusses many topics in general, to help you grasp the wide world of what's needed for success. The Resources Appendix listings are for complete, in-depth understanding of complex topics. It points to a lot of motivational advice as well (because writers need all the motivation they can get!), but more than just a positive attitude, you need positive *action*.

You may have comments after reading this book. At the end are a few questions for feedback, if you're so inclined to let me know what was useful and what could be improved. If future editions need something to make the book better for everyone, by all means, send it along.

Part One

Setting up the Mindset

Dale T. Phillips

The Changed World of Publishing

"In a time of drastic change, it is the learners who inherit the future. The learned usually find themselves equipped to live in a world that longer exists."

— Eric Hoffer

In the past, almost all professional fiction on the market went through publishers, who set all the terms. Because the costs of printing, distribution, and advertising were expensive, it was considered mutually beneficial— the publisher took the financial risks of printing mass "runs" of books and distributing them. They had to guess about the possibility of profit in each instance. It was expensive, and they were taking a chance, every time. One statistic said that out of every five books on average, one would turn a profit, two would break even, and two would lose money. So they bet on what they considered would sell. Trouble was, even when they still had people who knew books, they were wrong so much of the time— and yet still made money. When you've got a monopoly on production, you can profit, as there are few challenges.

Dale T. Phillips

Everything that didn't sell more expensive hardback copies was a heresy that traditional publishing fought. Cheaper paperback books were considered an abomination, yet readers loved them and bought even more books of all types, increasing readerships. Ebooks came along, and it was said they'd never be a significant part of the market (it's rather significant now). The concept of audiobooks was thought marginal, and now they're getting a bigger share of the market. At every turn, people found other ways of accessing stories without paying a lot for each one, yet with more profit to the creators— the authors. With each new method, smart authors could profit from adopting the path.

Still, printing books remained pricey until the advent of Print on Demand (POD) technology, where printing books became lower-priced, and one only needed to order as small a print run as they wanted— no more dozens of boxes of unsold books in the garage for the self-published! Ebooks were even cheaper, and they started getting a higher profile. "Self-published" for so long was synonymous with "trash," because anyone could do it, and it had not been blessed by the gatekeepers. Self-published authors were dismissed as hobbyists, not professionals. Yet some began creating works as good as the professionals, with astonishing results. Some sold primarily ebooks, and the early days of Kindle became a gold rush for a select few. Having quality items in a limited field can certainly be profitable, and many blasted out their results to upend the publishing world.

So the publishing world no longer belongs to the gatekeepers. It is possible to publish and sell without an agent or a publisher (middlemen between the author and reader), and to keep control of one's own work. It does mean that anyone wishing to be successful in this path learn a great deal about the ways and means of selling online, in essence becoming a small business. But a true business it can be.

So that's where we are today— any writer has multiple means of getting their stories out to the world without waiting years for a blessing or "go-ahead" from strangers. One can even make money at it, and some can even be very successful, by adopting techniques used by successful authors before them. The information is available because the Independent (Indie) community is very open and helpful, and willing to share what works.

The ones to be pitied are the traditional writers, who came of age in a system that may have worked for them in the past, but no longer works for most. While writing stays the same, many writers have quit, unable to deal with the changes to everything they knew about publishing, and unwilling to learn. The sad part is, even with traditional publishers they are now expected to do much of their own marketing and selling anyway, but they have many more restrictions, and must do it without many of the benefits that Indies enjoy. With the publishing world turned upside down, the Indies are now the ones with the best chances of success going forward.

Many traditional authors bewail people finding mistakes in their books, because it is expensive to change the galley proofs, so many errors remain unfixed. Indie writers can correct any published error and have an updated version in minutes, for ebooks, and days for print.

Why Go Indie

This section details why I decided to switch to Independent publishing, though I started out on a traditional path. It was after years of research: online, in print, and in person. I read books and articles and blogs on the new way publishing was changing. I attended writer conferences and spoke to many writers, who were uneasy or unhappy with traditional publishing, but afraid to risk their careers on something new and mostly untried. I studied those who were successful with the new methods of Indie, and modeled some of their techniques. I tested, liked the results, and went further.

Here's what I found out, as have many others: many of the "truths" of publishing are old myths, and the odds against being successful in traditional publishing were abysmally low. I gathered data, anecdotes and numbers. This section details some examples, in no particular order.

What mainly turned me off traditional publishing was the countless horror stories of bad agents, bad contracts, bad publishers, bad faith, bad experiences. Cheats, liars, and thieves. Court battles, broken promises, shattered careers, marriages, and lives. I didn't want to deal with any of that. With Indie, I didn't have to!

And the fact that once publishers get rights to your book, it's a battle to ever get them back. If the publisher screws up, or does nothing with the book, your work might get held up for years without seeing the light of day. They control everything from the cover, the content, the price, the publish date, the marketing, and so much of the time they can get it wrong. But no matter what, if the book doesn't sell, they'll always blame the writer. Always.

The music business provides a good model for study. For so long, the (only) way to success was to get signed by a big record company. Many artists did so and got completely screwed, desperately signing horrible contracts. Most bands and singles didn't do much past an album or two. Then the Indie music scene happened, and people didn't have to sign with someone who would control them and their career. Some made their own labels and did the music the way they wanted to. Companies care about control and profits, not people, not art.

Standard traditional book publishing practice is to give an *advance against future royalties* to get rights to a book. This money is paid in installments, and takes a long time to get. In most cases, it's not much, not enough to live on if one is only writing a book a year- and for the longest time, traditional publishing didn't usually publish more than that from a writer, not knowing the market. Many writers, even Stephen King had to publish extra books under pen names, because they had more output than the snail pace of traditional publishing allowed.

Even after publishers paid money and signed deals, many books never saw the light of day. Some publishing houses closed or merged, editors left, tastes or times changed. But once traditional publishing had the rights, writers were stuck, unable to have their work get to the public if the publishing house didn't follow through. One long-time, top best-selling, award-winning writer said that her book sat on someone's desk for *four years*! No thanks. Another had a book hang in unpublished Purgatory, even after collecting a six-figure advance for it!

The time between signing a deal to sell a book to a publisher (after the usual years to get an agent and get to that point) and publication is anywhere from months

Dale T. Phillips

to years. And getting paid royalties for the book takes even longer.

For many years, the "mid-list" authors were reliable sellers of a few thousand copies every year, as opposed to the "best-sellers". But traditional publishing started losing interest in writers who weren't best-sellers. Many writers were dropped, and lost their living as advances grew smaller and smaller. Traditional publishing stopped printing books which fell below the desired sales numbers. And so many books became "Out of Print" and unavailable, until the Print-on-Demand revolution, which made it possible to independently publish. Many good writers were suddenly and unceremoniously ditched by their publishers, and didn't know what to do next. I wanted my books to be always available, in all formats, so now I never have to worry about being dropped by my publisher for poor sales numbers.

Statistic: **Most books, about 95% or better, however published, do not sell more than a few hundred copies**.

I figured I could do better than that on my own.

How to Be a Successful Indie Writer

It was shocking to find out that on a $30 traditional publishing hardcover book purchased from a bookstore, the writer usually only made about a dollar or two. I couldn't afford many new hardbacks, and bought most books at discount venues, or in paperbacks, and used the free libraries. The authors would not see a profit from this. I'd gladly pay an author for good work, but refuse to pay a publishing company a lot to give the author so little. Ebooks changed that.

In one online forum exchange with the head of a publishing house, I pointedly asked why they couldn't pay authors more of a share of the profits. His claim was the high Manhattan-office costs, and that everyone else in the publishing business had to make a living. I chided him for his contention was that an author could starve, despite that they were the one providing support to many others. Entirely backward. Again, no thanks.

In the past, publishing yourself meant that you had to order a large number of books from a printer, which were hard to sell, and costly up-front. New POD technology meant one could order a few at a time, and so made it affordable to Indie publish. Ebooks didn't cost anything for printing, and so were pure profit. But traditional publishing felt that ebooks cut into the sacred paper sales, so they jacked up ebook prices (still do, in most cases), and often would not put out ebook versions until months after the hardcover (a process called windowing), frustrating many fans, who wanted the latest work *now*.

One panel of best-sellers at a conference all showed books that made a ton of money and topped the best-seller charts when they were finally published- but each book had been turned down an average of fifty times! I got to thinking that if an entire industry could not determine a good book when they saw it, why deal with them?

Here's just a few things that have changed.

•   Traditional publishing no longer equates to a reliable standard for quality. You can probably name several traditional publishing best-sellers that were howlingly bad. But readers wanted them, so traditional publishing made money off them. Having a book published by traditional publishing is no guarantee of a good production team, and often non-name writers get less-than-optimal results, from editing, to covers, to advertising, to all aspects. When many independent "writers" jumped on the easy-pub bandwagon and pushed out crap, critics used those as the typical examples, to demonstrate that all Indie was substandard. Yet many Indie writers produce high quality work.

• Bookstores are no longer the best places to sell books. Until the disruptive technology of online sales, they were, and the advantage was to traditional publishers. But ebooks (and Amazon) changed that, so that now a writer has a worldwide sales channel, working 24/7/365. Ebooks are cheaper, so more people can afford them, and buy more.

• Traditional publishing still has a seasonal cycle of releases, and any book that does not quickly hit with the public gets removed to make way for the next batch. Bookstore copies are stored mostly spine-out for about 90 days, amidst thousands of others, and gone after a few months, replaced by the next crop. An Indie writer can promote that same book for years, run occasional sales and specials, include it in bundles with other books and authors, and make money over and above what they would have received for an advance.

Resource Appendix: Jane Friedman details the pros and cons of Indie versus Traditional in excellent detail.

One link: https://createifwriting.com/traditional-publishing-indie-publishing/

Dale T. Phillips

What is Success?

"What's money? A man is a success if he gets up in the morning and goes to bed at night and in between does what he wants to do."
—Bob Dylan

What to know up front:

Success is not guaranteed. Luck is involved (next chapter)— but the harder you work, the luckier you usually get. Success becomes much more *probable*, even likely, if you *plan* for it, and constantly *work* for it. It will likely be hard, and won't come quickly, but your chances are good.

A short dictionary definition of success:

A person or thing that achieves desired aims or attains prosperity.

The outcome of an undertaking, specified as achieving its aims.

Yes, *achieving aims.*

Many people have the *desire* to write a book. They have a story to tell, whether it's the story of their life, someone else's, or something made up. Many talk about *wanting* to do it, *dream* of doing it, but they just never seem to make it enough of a priority to find the time or the impetus to put the butt in the chair and do the work. So they never achieve their aim. Or they get discouraged along the way. Winston Churchill said that success consists in going from failure to failure without losing enthusiasm, and who wants that?

This link was from an author who had 23 years of rejection!: https://www.pw.org/content/zen_and_the_art_of_qui cksand_my_twentythreeyear_descent_into_literary_fail ure_rejection_and

Almost everyone *thinks* they can write, they just need some big blocks of time, you know, like maybe after they retire, despite not having done it for their lives. Hey, they write emails all day, how hard can it be? We use the language every day, it's just a matter of recording words, right? Well, it's a lot more than that. Stephen King has a great cheeky response to the types of people who say they want to *write a book some day* (but never will). "Yes, and I've always wanted to try doing brain surgery some day."

Others make an actual start on a book. They get some words down on paper, almost always finding out that what is in the head is difficult to transfer clearly to the page. Many give up when they realize that finishing seems like an impossible task. I've known a number of talented writers who never got around to completing even one novel. It's a shame, really, because they had real skills in storytelling.

A few go on to finish a draft of a book. For most, that first one is a tough learning experience, the result is not very good, and is more of a home project than commercial material. It's difficult to create something wonderful when you're just learning how to do such a monumental creation project. But they *completed* a book, and that's a great step on the success path. Most writers will tell you of early novels of theirs that have never been published, because they were not good. Since the first novel or few is the learning part, many mistakes are made. The books produced are called "trunk novels" or "drawer novels," because one writes them, but they're so bad, they get stuck in a trunk or a drawer, and never see the light of day. The writers realize the (usually) low quality of that first production, and seek to do better. They'll learn more about the craft, and work on another book, using what they've learned. A few unwise ones will try to sell that first book, despite the flaws. Most will not have success at that, for obvious reasons. Fewer still will finish another book, and go on to publication eventually, and more books. And most published books do not sell more than a couple of hundred copies.

Statistic: Over 80% of published authors stop after 3 books. About 10% of published authors make it to six books. **Only 5% make it to twelve**.

This is a field in which, with practice and proper learning, one can develop skill enough to have a good product for sale. However, very few will continue for years to learn and grow and do better, because the financial rewards are usually small. They realize that for the time spent, they could make more money working a minimum-wage job. Writers do it for the love of what they're doing. Only a handful turn this quaint hobby from a dream into something more, and this book will hopefully inspire you to be one of those achievers. The level of success achieved depends in great part on the effort put out by the achiever. Those who produce good work, constantly learn more, and follow successful models should do well.

Dean Wesley Smith and his wife, Kristine Kathryn Rusch (see the Resources Appendix) have been professional writers for over forty years, and they've seen many people just give up writing, because they cannot sustain the success they desire. Most writers don't stick around long enough to write ten books, so if you do, congrats. My original plan was that when I had ten good published novels, ten story collections, and 100 published stories, I'd have a good start, and be a professional. I'm close to that goal now, though I've set further goals. I get to do what I want, on my schedule, and enjoy the results.

The Competition

There are millions of books out there, more than anyone can ever read. This is now a world of *infinite* free entertainment (including music, movies, television, etc.), so if a stranger gives you money for something you made up in your head, *you are a success!* No one *has* to read anything you wrote, or give you so much as a penny for it. The fact that anyone does means you're doing something right, that your stories matter enough to pay for.

Somebody said that the unsuccessful get halfway to the finish line and turn around. When the successful get halfway, they keep going. It's the same distance at that point.

Luck

The one thing as a writer to understand and accept: in reality, you have very little control over how many people will pay for your writing, or how many readers you will get. None. Advertising, quality, being deserving, *none* of it is a *guarantee* of sales. If your book sells, great, but even some of the great classics of the past were absolute failures in their time. Whether or not a book sells a lot of copies depends greatly on **LUCK**. Some of the worst books hit it big, and some of the best had original pitiable sales numbers, and were quickly forgotten. Some books were pushed hard by traditional publishing, with major sales campaigns, and they were still flops. Some were rejected to death, and others blew up out of nowhere and sold millions.

As best-selling mystery author Barbara Ross says: "*Even if you do everything right, you still might not move the sales needle significantly.*"

NOTE: Despite this hard, realistic fact, the more you *plan* and *work* for success, the more likely it becomes, as you increase your chances significantly. That's what this book is about.

How to Get Luckier

Richard Wiseman showed some research into how lucky people generate good fortune, via these basic principles:

- They are skilled at creating and noticing chance opportunities

- They make lucky decisions by listening to their intuitions

- They create self-fulfilling prophesies via positive expectations

- They adopt a resilient attitude that transforms bad luck into good

Low Sales

When authors whine about their low sales, one of my favorite examples to bring up is the artist Vincent Van Gogh. His paintings are worth uncounted millions now, and he is considered one of the most influential artists *of all time*. I ask the disgruntled author(s) how many paintings did Van Gogh sell in his lifetime of work? *One.* One painting, to his brother Theo, who had a *gallery*. Vincent's work was completely unappreciated in his time. And yet, he produced more and more work, keeping up his art without stopping. He *had* to paint. Some have to write. So I tell the author(s) if they've sold a single book to a stranger, *they've already been more successful in their lifetime* than Van Gogh was in *his*. Some of them really get it, and it's great to watch them process that, and change the frame of how they view their own success.

There is no telling what will happen to book sales over time. Some sell in small numbers but steadily over the years, some hit it big long after their publication date. Don Winslow is an astonishingly good writer, who toiled for twenty years with *meh* sales, until exploding with a best-seller. Philip K. Dick, the science fiction writer, had fairly modest sales in his lifetime, and now they're making smash movies and television shows from dozens of his works. Shame he didn't live to see it, he'd have been baffled and tickled at the same time. Emily Dickinson didn't have many poems published until after she was dead, and now she's a literary icon. You just never know when your work might get popular.

The thing is to *get it out*. An unpublished book does not sell, while each published work increases your chances of having more sales of *all* your work (**discoverability**). That's a term for when readers *discover* your work.

Dale T. Phillips

Some authors write a book, get it quickly published without the years of frustration and heartache, and do well right out of the gate. That's been the dream sold by traditional publishing for years, that once you're launched, you've made it. It's only true for a tiny few—like someone who doesn't usually play the lottery buying one ticket one day and hitting it big. Some friends of mine were a big deal starting with their first novel, and good for them, because they're terrific people and excellent writers. Another writer had written a novel, went to a party, mentioned his book, and got an agent essentially on the spot, and went on to a nice career writing mystery novels, without any of the hassle of agent and publisher hunting. He's careful about telling this story, because so many authors have gone through hell, and here he breezed past all that, and knows many would hate him for it. For some, it's difficult not to begrudge someone else's spectacular good fortune if you've been struggling to do something similar for years, but without success.

Getting lucky involves putting yourself in a position to recognize and act on the lucky breaks when they happen. The more you follow the success techniques, the more often you get a shot at lucky breaks. Funny thing is, even with those who seemed to have skipped the line, they were writing for years before they became an "overnight" success. When author B.A. Shapiro burst onto the scene with *The Art Forger*, most people didn't know she wrote *nine* novels before that, which didn't get sold or published, and she had all but given up— only convinced to do "one more" by her husband. So, for many, having an incredibly supportive spouse is one of those "lucky breaks"! Remember that Tabitha King pulled a few pages of beginner *Carrie* manuscript from the wastebasket, and convinced Stephen to continue with it! That one turned out rather well…

Another author who hit it big with traditional publishing on her first novel told me she'd written *twenty* unpublished novels before that. That's dedication to your craft, people, and that's how she got good enough to do well when the time came to go commercial. And yet, some authors still feel she didn't "pay her dues," and she has a tough time with the naked, bitter envy of those who haven't worked anywhere near as long or hard as she has.

So if you've written only one or two books or so, and haven't got them to the top of the *NY Times* best-seller list yet, don't despair. John D. MacDonald (or Ray Bradbury, or both) said that a writer has to write about a *million* words without any hope of selling them before they're good enough to really sell. That number is more than a lot of writers will ever do in their entire career. That's more than a dozen of those roughly 80K manuscripts that traditional publishing wants. If you only write one book a year, that's twelve years of unpaid work *before* you do your good work. How many are willing to undergo that long an apprenticeship, with no guarantee?

With the new world in Indie publishing, one can publish anything and everything they've written. Best though, is to polish your work before you show it to the world. Don't push out any old junk and expect it to sell a lot of copies. Too many did that (and still do), and it gives Indie a bad rap, giving fuel to those who only point out the worst examples as representative of the whole world of Indie.

If a book is poorly written or badly flawed, I seldom give that author another chance. This includes many of the authors I meet, and even though they're nice, and trying hard, I won't finish their book if it doesn't meet my standards for story and quality. The flip side is when I try something new and like it, I'll grab other books that author has written. Some people have read one of my mystery novels, liked it, and then bought the entire series. Good work has a much better chance of selling well. Sounds simple, but a surprising number of people don't want to do the hard work to make a book better. We had one such in a critique group, and we gave him terrific ideas which would make the story compelling and exciting, a simple change that would kick it from humdrum into high gear. He said he'd already written that section, so he didn't want to bother. His books do not sell well, and that's not bad luck, just poor craftsmanship.

For some authors who did well with their first novel, it put too much pressure on them to repeat, and they suffered from the 'Sophomore slump' of having trouble trying to make the next one as good. It even ruined some. If an author dumps their entire life story into the first book, what's left for them to write about, when the traditional publishing house wants another just like it?

In this new world, there's a related issue where authors who sold x number of copies in the past are selling thousands fewer with each book. Many writers who used to make a comfortable living can no longer sustain the sales numbers to pay the bills. That's usually due simply to the major paradigm shifts in the publishing world, but if some enjoyed a career of success that suddenly went away, some writers panic, or are at a complete loss as to how to proceed. They've never *had* to adapt, and now they must, if they wish to keep going. As Dean Wesley Smith and Kristine Kathryn Rusch have extensively documented, they know of many writers who simply gave up because they could not sustain their past sales numbers. Add to that the declining advance offers, and the hundreds of authors dropped by their publishers, and you've got big problems for many.

You know the publishing world has changed when long-time writers with distinguished careers, a string of awards, and track records of outstanding success are coming up to *me* (and Indie authors like me) to ask for advice on how now to move forward with their writing career. And yes, it happens more often than you'd think. Some get it, and are willing to adapt, others just quit, because it's difficult and all new territory.

In poker, we have a half-joking saying: *It's better to be lucky than good.* But don't just put out something and hope for good luck. In writing, the better you are, and the more you work for it, the better your chances of good luck allowing you to sell more.

The Big Break

One day, something big might fall in your lap: the big contract, the television or movie option, the promotion that sells thousands. Celebrate, enjoy thoroughly, and also use caution. The wonderful wave might be a temporary thing, so never assume good fortune will last forever. There have been too many articles by authors who got a whopping book contract for a truckload of money, thought they *Had it Made*, spent the money, and found out the gravy train wasn't running much after that. Some even got themselves into serious financial trouble, which is why you need that business way of thinking (later in this book). They'd spend that windfall without taking care of the bottom line, and before they knew it, they'd overextended. The luck which seemed fabulous now looked like a curse.

And sometimes the big break is only *promised*, such as getting a movie or television deal, which may take years, or not come to fruition at all, through any number of things. That's happened to a few writer friends, who have seen lovely offers come and go. It's frustrating to have the big brass ring within reach, only to have it snatched away. Don't spend money that isn't in your account yet!

Fortune's Wheel turns: one day you have great reviews, interviews aplenty, award nominations, top placement on selling charts, and everything going right. A few years later, it seems you can't sell anything, nobody knows your name, and you're left wondering what happened. Don't get discouraged, it's just life. Keep on the success path for a continued career.

The Secret Formula

A few short stories and a novel or two (even if sold to a major publisher) is not usually enough for a career. Making the equivalent salary of a full-time job year after year is really hitting the lottery, and quite an achievement. Sales and writing income fluctuate wildly, and one must plan carefully if this is the main source of income. One research data point said that most Indie fiction writers making an average of 5000 dollars a month have a number of things in common:

• Average of 13.5 books published, mostly with series, and popular genres.

• Good content, formatting, editing, covers, pricing, availability.

• Good connection with followers on social media and via email lists.

It's the combination of things, not just one single thing. Achieve all this, and you'll likely be quite successful:

• Do your research

• Set reasonable expectations

• Make plans with achievable goals

How to Be a Successful Indie Writer

- Work with decent levels of diligence, skill and persistence

- Continue to walk the success path.

Each opportunity, done well, creates more and better opportunities. Each thing you do well puts you further ahead, and there are no limits to what you can achieve.

Critics abound, regretfully. There will be people who tell you that it's not possible to be successful at Indie writing, that you'll never make a fortune, *you'll never* yadda, yadda, yadda. They may be sincere, but they also may be misinformed, or simply not acting in your best interests. Eliminate negative voices from your circle— you don't want them taking up space in your head. Writers are their own self-negating voices, and need no additional negativity from anyone else. Many people who accomplished great things had others telling them that they wouldn't or couldn't. Ignore the critics, and make it happen. Just don't feel you have to learn and do it all at once. It's a process, and a long road. Take your time and enjoy the journey. Laugh at your mistakes, they're part of your story. Build a strong foundation for continued success.

Success is a house you build yourself, so it's up to you what it looks like and how comfortable you are with it. Others aren't going to build it for you, but this book points you to the tools you'll need. Use the right materials, and take your time to build well.

The Big Secret

The main thing I discovered, after all this time, is that because success takes a lot of hard work, most people just don't want to do it. They'll make *some* effort, and hope for lightning to strike, but won't do the *sustained* effort it takes. Yet all the successful Indie writers do the work necessary to make it.
That's really the big secret.

Steps to success:

• Always be learning. Learn what marketing steps other people have taken to improve their income and craft, then copy or improve on those steps and repeat

• Set realistic goals, plans, and schedules

• Try a lot of approaches and ideas new and old

• Keep at different methods until something works

• Study to see if the methods can be made more effective

• Absorb feedback and cycle through until success is the result

• Celebrate each success, then move on to the next thing

Write well, learn the craft, publish, follow the plans for success, and things could work out very well indeed for you. If sales are always poor over time, it might be something other than luck. Get the advice of people who've been doing this for a while and know about the new world of Indie publishing. Consider what you have for offerings.

• Are you doing what you should?

• Are your books in a popular genre and well-written?

• Are the covers good?

• Are the books priced properly?

• Are they available in different formats with different distributors?

• Does your platform support enough promotion about it?

Dale T. Phillips

Staying Motivated

"People of mediocre ability sometimes achieve outstanding success because they don't know when to quit. Most people succeed because they are determined to. Persevere and get it done."

—George Allen

Think of it this way: Failure is a *single* event, while success is a *process*.

You should realize (if you hadn't before) that the road to success is a long, constant journey, not a short sprint to a nearby finish line. Many writers quit before achieving success, including some who were close and would have made it with just a bit more effort. You never know how close you are, where the tipping point will be. In the past couple of years, two of my favorite writers suddenly broke into top-level, best-seller, well-deserved, breakout success after many years of toiling in the trenches. It seemed to happen overnight, and yet they'd been working diligently for years to make it happen, and had a number of excellent books out.

How to Be a Successful Indie Writer

Sure, if you're not having fun, and it's taking a toll on your life, it may not be the thing you think you wanted. But if you have that need to write, to get your stories out to the world, you'll keep going. How does one persist when success seems unobtainable? One book I highly recommend is *Motivate Your Writing!: Using Motivational Psychology to Energize Your Writing Life*, by Stephen Kelner. He's also married to a writer, so he knows his stuff.

Before my first novel was published, I was chomping at the bit to get my book out. It seemed just out of reach for several years, and I had to prod myself to keep going. One Christmas I printed out the book draft, stuck the pages in a large binder, wrapped it, and gave it to myself as a wonderful Christmas gift. Though my family thought it strange, it was terrific motivation, and gave me a boost to continue thinking about the day when I would hold a real print copy of my first novel. That day came, and many more of amazing success. This last Christmas, I had three unfinished novels and another I wanted to write, and hadn't published enough work in too long a while. So I printed title covers, attached them to other books, wrapped them, and gave them to myself as more gifts, as a promise and a commitment that I'd get to work and finish and publish them. Then, despite the plague that arrived to disrupt the world, I'm well on my way to completing that goal.

I'm motivated by the stories of amazing writers (and other artists, musicians, entertainers, and creative people) of talent who had a much tougher time of it, who struggled to get published and make a living in years past. Now we can get published whenever we want, but the hard part is getting sold and read. Inspirational quotes and success stories help keep me going. I look outside writing, to success and motivation gurus, to see if I can use techniques for success from other walks of life. By keeping a positive attitude, you can push through the dark days. The habit of success keeps you on track when you encounter setbacks. Do not allow events to stop you. Learn the power of the word NO when asked for things that will suck up your time if they prevent you from finishing projects.

Stories

One way I get quick jolts of renewed energy and motivation along the road is by writing and selling short stories. Completing a good story is another badge of success, and selling that story is a major accomplishment. They can be done quickly in many cases, a nice break from the long slog of completing a novel. Month after month of rewrites and edits and worrying about deadlines can be worse than tedious, and a nice short story sale can lift you up during the tough times. Few things motivate me more than getting notice of another story acceptance while I'm struggling to churn out the word count or fix a complicated timeline or plot on a longer work.

Writing sellable short stories will also make you a better writer. In short, focused bursts, you boil a tale down to the essence of storytelling, keeping only the things that matter. Following the advice of Elmore Leonard, you leave out the parts that people skip (which many novel writers need to heed). You also follow the guidelines of Edgar Allen Poe (who knew a few things about successful short stories), who argued that every word in a short story (which should be read in a single sitting) should go for that final, telling effect. The short story cannot afford the bloated excess of some novels, with superfluous characters, plotlines that meander, and meaningless side-notes. By writing good short stories (which will also be the ones that sell), your writing sharpens to the crisp and specific.

You can also get out of your rut and take risks with a short story, writing in different genres, writing experimental work, and mashing up genres. Have some fun with it. Maybe it's time to write that Chupacabra time-travel romance tale. Give it a shot, because someone may love what you come up with. You may get creative in ways that will pay off down the road in other works.

Another good motivator is the compensation. As Dorothy Parker once wrote: "The two most beautiful words in the English language: *Check enclosed.*" While it may not pay off the mortgage, a successful sale can keep the lights on. And you can get more than a one-time sale for first North American serial rights, too. You can sell the tale as reprints to other markets, to be included in anthologies, and bundled into your own collections for sale. You can publish short stories and put them up for sale on different sites. Dean Wesley Smith actually tells how you could even make a living by writing and selling nothing but short stories.

More motivation is the exposure and promotion you get from having your work read by hundreds or thousands that may not have seen your novels. Why pay to take out an ad for your work when they'll pay *you* to have your own work promoting you in the magazine? The circulation of the published venue is a whole crop of potential new fans who might seek out your other writing. To this day, I remember my first Ray Bradbury story, as well as never being able to forget the chill of Shirley Jackson's *The Lottery*. And I sure looked up their other works as fast as I could after reading those stories.

How to Be a Successful Indie Writer

By adding to your body of work, your intellectual property, you increase the chances of a bigger score: television, movies, or more. Elmore Leonard went from a short story *Fire in the Hole* to the *Justified* television series expanding from it. Daniel Keyes wrote *Flowers for Algernon*, and it morphed into a novella, a play, and then a movie (*Charley*, with Cliff Robertson). Practically a career out of one story.

So treat yourself to an enjoyable day trip every now and then. Don't worry about the market, write from your passion and the things that intrigue and scare you. Write the kind of short story you love to read. Only when it's done do you concern yourself with where to sell it. And don't get discouraged if it doesn't click right away. One of my most successful stories was turned down over thirty times, while the penciled notes from editors kept calling it *brilliant, clever, whimsical*. When it finally found a home, it was a big hit, and I heard good things from readers, including a request for more like it!

Dale T. Phillips

Part Two

Setting up the Foundation

Dale T. Phillips

Starting

Some of the basic questions a starting writer has:

- *How do I write?*

- *What do I write?*

- *How do I publish?*

- *How do I promote and sell?*

How Do I Write?

"If you don't have time to read, you don't have the time (or the tools) to write. Simple as that."

— Stephen King

King is right on this. To be successful in selling the written (fictional) word, you really must be in love with *reading.* You've got to know how words are put together to make a compelling story, you've got to know what works in telling a story, and what doesn't work. You've got to know the field you're competing in. If you write in a genre, you must know the tropes and conventions of that genre. Storytellers enjoy the stories of others, and learn from them. Walking through a house frame doesn't make you a carpenter, it's having the tools and skills and experience to know how things are put together. As a master carpenter is a craftsman, making things fit, functional, and looking good, so must you be with your writing.

You don't need a college degree, or specialized training. While it's helpful to improve through workshops, writing programs, mentoring, critique groups, you can learn much on your own through focused study and practice, practice, practice. Always be improving. The more you write, the better you should get, because the study and the practice works to improve what you do. The "Ten-thousand-hour rule" is much more complex than just putting in that number of hours to get successful. You need specific, focused practice.

There are hundreds of books that tell you how to become a better writer, and they can be your writing program. You should be familiar with at least some of the best of them (listed in the Resources Appendix), and absorb their lessons. See what the writers you admire recommend. Every year, you should have gone through some craft lessons that will make your writing better. Even now, I'll come across some piece of advice that helps me get unstuck from some thorny issue I'm having with the telling of a tale. These are tips from professional writers who've been there, and most of your issues will have been discussed somewhere. Having a broad and deep knowledge of the lessons of the writing craft books is a substantial help in becoming a successful Indie writer.

Are you familiar with how tales are told in different Points of View (POV)? Story arcs? The hero's journey? Beats in story structure? The unreliable narrator? Foreshadowing? The surprise ending or twist? All this and more should be part of your craft knowledge.

The answer to when to write is whenever you can, and whatever works for you: morning, noon, night, lunch breaks, vacations, whenever. Having the habit of daily writing is supreme, because it makes you practice a lot, which gets you better quicker, and produces more output. A mere 500 words a day, most days, gives you the word count of several novels in the course of a year. Don't wait for the perfect time or for inspiration, they may not come as often as needed. Put words down as often as possible, even if they're not good. They'll get better.

What Do I Write?

Dale T. Phillips

The question of *what* to write is a personal one. Some
writers set about creating books for the market they
think are popular types, chasing the latest publishing
fad. This rarely works in traditional publishing, because
the long development times mean the fad will likely be
over by the time the book is ready to come out, or the
fad too quickly gets glutted with similar books. The best
thing about Indie publishing is you never have to worry
that a particular book won't get published, due to it not
being commercial enough for someone else to make a
lot of money from.

Traditional path writers have to constantly worry about
being dropped by their publisher if a book doesn't sell
well, so they strive to be as commercial as possible.
While they do, there's usually the desire to write "the
book of the heart," one that matters to them, but may
not be as commercially successful. In the Indie world,
every book can be the book of the heart. And when you
write books that deeply matter to you, you'll likely find
a devoted readership, and more personal success, rather
than writing blah books you don't care about, even if
they put food on the table. My metaphor for this is that
fast-food chains make money selling a lot of junk food,
which fills a need for many. I prefer to run a top-level
restaurant, which produces memorable meals that
create a good life experience.

How Do I Publish?

To the question of *how* to publish, this book has some thoughts, and points toward many more resources that break down the process into far more detail. Because there are now different, good options, each writer must decide what path is best for themselves.

There's a lot to learn about the world of publishing these days. Lucky for you, there's a great deal of good information about at your fingertips, distilled down for you to easily absorb. If you want to be successful, it's good to know what's happening in the writing and publishing world. The Resources Appendix has some sites you'll definitely want to be familiar with, as they detail aspects of what's happening. Various articles, blogs, and newsletters give great information on current writing and publishing events. Writer organizations let their members know about areas of concern. Some sites warn of various dangers, such as predatory people or trends. Be aware of your world.

Publishing in general:

- Research! Learn the business before you publish.

- Go Indie to control your career.

- Go wide for Discoverability (how can readers find your books?)- Formats, Distributors, and promote for free in as many places as you can.

- All formats- print, ebook, audio, others as they become available.

- Use the big distributors- Amazon/Ingram's Lightning Source for print, Smashwords/Draft2Digital for ebooks, and options like ACX/Audible for audio.

How Do I Promote and Sell?

To the question of how to promote and sell, there are hundreds of books which go into great detail about how to do just that. You should have at least a basic understanding of what's involved, and decide how much you want to take on versus how much time you have to write. Remember **WIBBOW**, which stands for *Would I Be Better Off Writing?*

It's going to take some work, because you're competing against millions of other books, many of them quite good. What's going to set your above the others, to make people want to *pay money* for yours? You won't have time or energy to do every darned thing. But the more you do, the better your chances.

How to Be a Successful Indie Writer

Some writers have expectations of huge sales with their first or second books. While it does happen from time to time (lottery wins), it's not a reasonable goal. Mostly a readership has to be built over time. *Up to 96% of all books don't sell more than a few hundred copies.* So anytime you meet or beat that average, you're a success! Study the concept of the Long Tail for an idea of how your work might grow over time.

If your view of success is limited simply to how much money you're making in the short term, you'll probably never be happy or successful enough. Human greed and desire is bottomless. In the words of robber-baron millionaire John D. Rockefeller, when asked how much money would make him happy: *"Just a little more* [but to infinity]."

Think of your writing career as a Johnny Appleseed metaphor, where each book is a single tree planted, each copy an apple from that tree. It takes time, and it's tough to make a living selling apples off just one tree. But if you've created an orchard, with quality and quantity, word will eventually get around. And you don't have to stick with just apples: you can sell cider, jelly, pies, all other formats. Continuing that metaphor, give people who haven't tried your product a free taste, because you know it's good, and they'll be back for more. Give copies away, so they'll find your other work.

Ebooks made this easy and free. Writers get more well known when their books are read for free in libraries. For the most part, forget about "piracy": superstar author Neil Gaiman talks a lot about being pirated, and giving away his work for free, and watching his sales go up!

There are still articles published saying how expensive it is to self-publish. If you pay too much for the many services available, it certainly can cost a lot. But there are so many free tools and inexpensive methodologies that you don't need to spend a lot of money. Do your homework!

So those are your expectations. Are you still ready to tackle this venture?

Legal Matters

Important: This work does not substitute for the advice of a professional attorney versed in these matters. In all legal affairs, get the advice of a professional experienced and licensed in said legal matters. Consulting with an attorney to do the proper things is far better than making assumptions or working from bad or incomplete advice, and getting into legal trouble later in your career, and losing money or rights, or undergoing a long court battle.

Always do your research first, especially in legal matters. There is so much arcane legal information when money is exchanged that we don't know about. Good intentions count for little when dealing with courts and attorneys. And the burden of proof over what was said or understood is difficult. When you do get financially successful, there may be people who try to carve themselves a slice of that from your earnings. Cover yourself from a legal perspective at all times. Most of the subjects in this chapter require much more understanding than what is presented here. They are brought up for reference, so you have starting points for going further.

Intellectual Property

Understand what Intellectual Property represents, and the vast scope of what can be done with it. Whatever you create out of your original ideas, and commit to a representational form, is your intellectual property. It has value. You may license off rights to use it in various degrees, for profit. The great thing is, you can do this over and over for different formats, when done right. Neil Gaiman licensed one work as a story, a book, a play, a radio reading, an audiobook, a television show, and a movie! All separate pieces, all creating a different income stream. Dean Wesley Smith did something similar with one single story being resold and repackaged many times to make thousands of dollars.

Subsidiary rights have value. When a traditional publisher licenses your book rights, many times most, if not all, of the subsidiary rights become theirs as a part of the contract. It's called "rights grabs," and it's becoming more prevalent, because they understand the potential value of these rights, in case anything becomes a hit, and they can leverage that intellectual property into greater sales of auxiliary material. They paid dearly for not paying attention to ebook rights, as many authors signed contracts before ebooks were a thing, and were thus able to get their own separate licensing for their ebook versions. Now there's legalese in the traditional publishing contracts for rights not even thought of yet. Use caution before signing it all away.

You may not think your property has much value, but there have been many breakout surprises.

For example, foreign rights, translations, and more. Your work might go to other countries and be translated into other languages. Each separate language can be a separate licensing piece, and there are a lot of languages. Although you may not get a shot at this unless you're selling a lot, or have a good sales record, it may arise in your career. You'll definitely need good advice on this to ensure it's a good thing.

Or you may create characters and stories that offer merchandising opportunities. This can be ridiculously lucrative, as George Lucas and many others discovered. Action figures, graphic novels made from your work, T-shirts, music! The possibilities are many.

Copyright

To be a successful writer, Indie or otherwise, you need to have a good understanding of copyright, and what that means for your work, because assumptions can be dangerous. A search on "Books on Copyright" will show dozens of options. Proving something in court can be a difficult endeavor, so for your works, register with the Copyright office.

Dale T. Phillips

https://www.copyright.gov/registration/literary-works/

One of the biggest reasons for going Indie is keeping control of your copyrighted material. When you sign with a publisher, you are licensing the copyright through them, and you cede control over it, in exchange for payment.

Think of it as having that orchard you own and cultivate. Each crop, you sell some of the fruit, but you keep the orchard going. You get to decide how to grow and sell the fruit. You spend years and a lot of hard work getting it right. Signing with a publisher is like selling the rights to the orchard. You'll still do all the work, but they'll tell you what to grow, how to grow it, when to pick it, and what to sell it for. Which would you rather do? An Indie *has* control, an agency writer *is controlled*— there's the difference.

Copyright is for life- your author life, anyway, plus 70 years. That's a long enough time to profit. You and your heirs can keep selling that crop year after year, provided you keep the rights to it. Or you can sell the control of the orchard, if the price is right. Your call.

There are pirate sites and scammers who will take your work and publish it as their own. Follow best practice for protecting yourself. There's Fair Use, and there's outright stealing. Know the difference. It's essential to post a copyright notice at the front of each book, something along the following lines:

All Rights Reserved. No part of this book may be reproduced in any form or by any means, electronic or mechanical, including photocopying, recording or by any information storage and retrieval systems, without the written permission of the copyright owner or the publisher.

Examples

Here are a couple of examples to illustrate the importance of *proving* copyright, and why your work belongs to you, and others must ask— or pay for the use of that.

Author Tess Gerritsen wrote a book called *Gravity*, about a doctor stranded in space. It was later made into a movie, which proved successful. Here's the story:

https://www.tessgerritsen.com/gravity-lawsuit-affects-every-writer-sells-hollywood/

The second example is the successful movie *The Terminator*, made by Director James Cameron. Here's a great explanation of that one:

https://electricliterature.com/was-1984s-the-terminator-a-harlan-ellison-rip-off/

There's a type of writing called *fanfiction*, or fanfic, where someone writes in a world already created by someone else, usually something popular. Always use caution, and carefully research all the rules for doing so. It's tough to get paid for this, since the original concept belongs to someone else, but a writer can get a huge following: I've known two good fanfic writers, both with over 100,000 followers: one was a high-school girl, and the other transitioned to commercial fiction.

Some writers work in a licensed *Shared World* environment, creating separate stories whose original concept was created by someone else. As always, tread carefully if you enter into an agreement for this, and know your legal rights and obligations.

Contracts

This cannot be stressed enough: **learn the importance of a contract**. Whatever is written down in it and agreed to can be enforced by the courts, even if it wasn't what you thought you were getting.

Remember, agents do not usually have law degrees- so if you're looking to them for legal advice, you're in trouble. First, they're practicing law without a license, so they're already breaking the law in many cases. They'll say they understand everything, or they had their agency attorney look it over and approve it.

Second, *it is in the agent's financial interest to have you sign a publishing contract, even if the terms are not as beneficial to you.* If you refuse to sign a publishing contract, the agent doesn't get paid, and they may have put in significant work to get to that point. An old proverb says that it is difficult to get someone to understand something when their income depends on them *not* understanding it. To them, even a bad contract might be better than none, but you could be the one stuck with terrible terms for a good part of your career. Numerous examples abound, as they also do in the music industry, a good parallel to publishing.

Third, publishing contracts are heavily weighted in favor of the publisher. Whoever writes up the contract does so for terms that primarily benefit *them*. You may find you're giving away the farm, for scraps. They have teams of attorneys creating these contracts, and have tacked on many additional rights grabs. You are at a major disadvantage, because you want so desperately to be signed, and saying *no* will set you back on your path.

So for any significant contract, have it vetted by an Intellectual Property Attorney (not just at the agency of your agent). It will cost you money, maybe around $300-$500 or more to get the contract inspected, and they will break the contract down and tell you what it really says. You'll likely be surprised. Many clauses are buried, and some parts of the contract negate other parts.

Disregard anyone who says "*Oh, that's just our standard contract boilerplate- it doesn't mean anything, so don't worry, we never really enforce it.*" Any time you sign, you are agreeing to whatever it says in that paper, so you jolly well better understand and approve each and every clause, or it could cost you a great deal of time, money, and frustration.

But my agent/publisher would never… Okay, suppose *they* wouldn't ever have you sign something that might come back to screw you later. Then what happens if the publisher is acquired by someone else, or your agent is replaced at the agency, and things get worse? People and jobs change, contracts can be forever.

Whenever you consider working with someone else where money will be involved, always consider having all parties sign a contract. It's protection for everyone, and a key ingredient in this modern litigious world.

Liability

Few people want to get sued. So for every work we create and publish, it's necessary to do at least the bare minimum of butt-covering, and that entails putting something along the lines of this disclaimer at the front of every book:

This is a work of fiction. Names, characters, places, and incidents are products of the author's imagination or are used fictitiously. Any resemblance to actual events, locales, or persons is entirely coincidental.

For non-fiction, add something like the following:

The publisher and the author make no guarantees concerning the level of success you may experience by following the advice and strategies in this book, and you accept the risk that results may differ for each individual. Neither the publisher nor the author, nor their heirs, shall be liable for any loss of profit or any damages, including but not limited to special, incidental, consequential, personal, or other damages.

Here's a great article on the subject:

https://www.janefriedman.com/5-things-nonfiction-authors-can-get-sued/

• For fiction, don't put recognizable people from your life into your work without their permission.

• In non-fiction, use care in how you use actual people and places. Some people have even been sued for reviews of places they posted online.

• Be careful with song lyrics, as quoting more than a few words can open you up to someone wanting money for your inclusion of those words. All quotes of more than a few words from a published work should be carefully checked for Fair Use. Do the research first.

https://writingcooperative.com/what-you-must-know-to-include-song-lyrics-in-your-story-96f69a79c75b

• If using real people, know about these terms, and tread carefully: Defamation, Right of Privacy, and Right of Publicity.

- Trademarks are legally-protected branding, so always use care when including references to trademarked items.

There's always a risk with anything that goes out to the world. You must weigh the risks, and there may be risks you don't know about. Fall back on the old saying:

When in doubt, leave it out.

Forming a Company

This topic will be explained in the Part Three, in the section *Setting Up the Business*.

Work For Hire

You may get a gig to create a work for someone else, where they'll pay you to create, but they own all the rights. You'll usually sign a contract that specifies the details. This can include ghost writing, and many other types. Do some background research to see if the time and effort is worth it, for something you may not get much (if any) credit for.

I declined one offer to write a popular series book, even though I loved the original from many years before. It would have been fun, but I decided the meager pay for six months of writing time and not being able to put my name on the cover wasn't worth it.

Working with Others

You may find yourself teaming up with one or more writers. This can be fun and rewarding, or a nightmare, and anything in between. Think carefully before jumping in and sharing credit with others. People who are your dear and trusted friend one day might not be in the future (yes, this happened to me), and the situation can get sticky rather fast. Some people like being in a band, some prefer to be a solo act. Dividing the money is a real pain, especially because it can come in such small amounts, and you have to keep track.

Always have a contract to spell out the details.

Great advice here once more from Jane Friedman. Working with others- https://www.janefriedman.com/author-collectives-coops/

After You're Gone- Your Estate

Perhaps you don't want to think about this, but preparation can save your heirs much grief, some sleepless nights, and a great deal of money. Not having your estate in order means that everything you worked for will go to a couple of law firms instead of people you care for. In the past year or two, there have been well-publicized cases of talented stars leaving huge estates in absolute disastrous array that will take years and millions of dollars to sort out.

Create a **Final Letter** that tells your heirs what they can, and should, do with it once they have it. You will need to organize your literary estate and educate your heirs, as in something like the following:

Dear Heir, What you need to understand is more than how to work with Copyright Law. You need to understand that **Intellectual Property** *can be immensely valuable. Not only can it be nearly infinitely subdivided, but it also has immense longevity. A house or condo ages. IP typically remains protected by Copyright Law in the US (and most places worldwide) for seventy years past the death of the author. Well-managed IP may not only support your children and grandchildren, but maybe even their children's children.*

As a holder of IP, you and your heir must be aware that you can't declare bankruptcy— ever. Why? Because the bankruptcy courts view IP as an asset of the estate. The court will seize these assets and sell them off to the highest bidder, often for cents on the dollar, and all of that potential future income will be lost and you'll never get it back.

There was a company that provided a Terms Of Service agreement for print distribution of an author's own book. For years the agreement included five separate documents that spanned over 120 pages of dense legalese. There were clauses that appeared to allow them the right to copy your book for free if they wanted to. In other words, if your book took off and became a huge success, they could sell their own copy of your book and never have to pay you a penny.

Setting up a trust is a big-time consult with a lawyer. If your estate is small, it may not be worth setting up a trust, because they cost money, may require additional tax filings, and more. How do you know how small is small? This takes work, and responsibility, and not everyone is up to the task. If it's more trouble than it's worth, so be it.

Here are some considerations:

• Passwords— Can your heirs find your passwords and all accounts?

• Money

• Vocabulary

• Remembering the importance of IP and different ways to manage it

• CPAs

• Lawyers

- Trusts

- Copyright Law

How to communicate all this to your heirs? The first step in communicating your estate to your heir: *Be Organized.*

Contents

- Introduction

- Where can they find the key stuff?

- Will, trust, accounts, bank books

- Knowing the terms

- Basic publishing education

- Where's the money?

- Where can they find everything else?

- All the publishing details

- Master file explanations

Dale T. Phillips

Agents- You Don't Need Them

In the past, literary agents were sometimes useful and
necessary for selling a manuscript to a publisher, and as
an author representative, negotiating a better deal for
the author for the sale of the book rights. Unsolicited,
un-agented manuscripts were often sent to the
publishing house. These were called *over the transom* (the
crossbar above a door), because in the olden days, some
were literally pushed through the window portion over
the transom in the hopes that someone would read
them. They would be dumped into a *slush pile*, and good
luck to anything that broke out of that oubliette. Once
in a great while, somebody would scan some of the
manuscripts in the pile and find a pearl in that
mountain of clamshells (not even oyster), and a miracle
occurred, and the book got published. Extremely low
odds, but it didn't stop the flow. Hope springs eternal
in the hearts of writers.

In the latter part of the twentieth century, the
publishing houses churned in a frenzy of consolidation
and mergers. The people taking them over were
interested in profits more than literature, and things
changed dramatically. Many people who had been in
the business for the love of books went away
(voluntarily or just cut), and the ones remaining had to
do more with much less. One thing that got outsourced

was the discovery of buyable manuscripts. Many publishers announced they would not accept unsolicited manuscripts. Some still did, even though they advertised the opposite. They just didn't want to deal with what they considered were piles of junk. So they pushed the work of editors and screeners onto literary agents, who would take on the burden of sifting through submissions for the needle in the haystack, the sellable manuscript. Agents became the gatekeepers to the Big Leagues- if you didn't have an agent, you couldn't even get someone to read your work. Agents were convenient for traditional publishing, because they'd recommend manuscripts that had some merit. If an agent sent nothing but duds, they wouldn't be around long.

Generalization follows. Agents screen by what they think will sell to the handful of editors they have contact with. And instead of reading actual manuscripts to start, they rely on the *query letter* from hopeful authors. A (usually) one-page letter is a summary of what the book is about. It can be scanned rapidly, and usually discarded. Their reasoning is that if a writer cannot write a good query, the manuscript isn't likely to be good. So now New Author must spend a lot of time composing the Perfect Query, all to hunt for the elusive Great Agent, who will take them on, to find the Perfect Publisher. Trouble is, the Great Agents are all booked up, and few are taking on new clients. Guess where that leaves New Author? Going through listing of potential agents to query, studying what kind of book they prefer to represent, and firing off a batch of queries to the selected group. Why in batches? Because the agents then usually take their sweet time about responding, if they respond at all. It can be days, but is more often weeks or months before the author hears back. And the response is usually *"Thanks, but it's not for us."*

How does one find a good agent that will take them on? At this point, it's a matter of rare good fortune. While there are excellent agents, there are some who are just awful, and a portion who are downright toxic or even criminal. Some famous authors have struck deals with well-bespoken top agents, only to discover horrendous abuses. See the horror stories of Laura Resnick and Kristine Kathryn Rusch. Sometimes the agents wouldn't bother notifying the author of additional potential deals. A bad decision by an agent can be costly. And that's just the honest ones! But new writers are so desperate to get an agent (a process that can often take *years*) that they'll sign with the first one who indicates interest. It can be a catastrophic mistake.

The problem is that anyone can say they're an agent, hang out an agent shingle tomorrow, run an ad or two, and within a few weeks, probably have hundreds of submissions, because there are so many people hungry for traditional publishing that they'll sign with anyone who'll take them. They'll be taken, all right, usually to the cleaners.

Agents need no certification or education, no degree, no proof of ability, no license, no standards. It's all voluntary. In many cases, they give legal advice on complex contracts (which benefit themselves)- in other words, *practicing law without a law license*, which is actually a crime. Thousands of authors hand over their careers and money to absolute strangers, with little or no vetting other than they saw a listing somewhere. And then a few emails and a phone call or two. *"They seemed nice, and eager to work with me."*

The publishing houses mostly send the money due the author for advances and royalties to the agent/agency. When does the author get paid? At the whim of the person holding the money. Imagine if your employer sent your paycheck to your bank, who then decided when and how much to give you of the money you'd earned!

It's always a good practice to be in charge of your own finances. If you *do* decide to sign with an agent, try to work it so the payments from the publishing house go to you first, or to each their share. After all, the agent is supposed to be working *for you*. Then *you* pay the *agent*. Unusual, but not unheard of.

Other problems with agents are that if you decide to part ways, you might still have to pay them *forever* for any of your books they represented, or even any you sold elsewhere while you were signed with them. Yup, you could wind up forking over your 15%, even *twenty years after you got rid of them*. Worse than alimony. And if they sold anything of a series, they may try to get a cut of any future books you sell from that series, even after you're no longer working together. Dean Wesley Smith says writers don't need agents anymore. He says it's like giving fifteen percent of your house value to the person who cuts your lawn.

Many authors say they love their agent. Some authors don't want to talk about bad experiences with agents, for fear they'll be blacklisted, because the Manhattan book world is a tiny bubble. And it's possible an author might not even know for a long time they're being badmouthed in the industry, and why doors are closed in their face. But many more will tell of the hell they went through with agents. One well-known example had an author finding out only *years later* that their agent had died!

If you want to work with an agent, be careful. Have any contract with the agent and with a publisher additionally vetted by qualified, licensed Intellectual Property attorneys, not just agents who say they know what they're doing. In the new world of publishing, agents are far less useful than they used to be. With all the changes, it's getting tougher for them to make a decent living as well. Not having an agent means not having to give up a good chunk of profits, which are slim enough.

However, if you *want* to meet agents, writer conferences are the best places, because many agents go there to find new clients, and expect to get pitched. Some agents even schedule *pitch sessions* at these conferences, where a prospective writer has a few minutes to pitch the agent on a book proposal. Many writers get asked for part or all of a manuscript, based on those few minutes. At least the agent will give it a chance.

If you do this, have a killer tagline to catch their interest. Follow with a few sentences similar to a description of other books the agent has done, or top-sellers. Think high-concept: for example, *Gone Girl* crossed with *Silence of the Lambs*, that sort of thing. Keep it simple, exciting, and show you know the marketplace and what type of book that agent represents. Most have their likes and dislikes available on their website, so do your homework first. Some give precise guidelines for how to pitch them. Don't think your manuscript is so wonderful that a strictly children's author representative will suddenly want your adult science fiction novel (yes, this kind of idiocy still happens). But if your book is like others the agent has represented, say so.

Your pitch could go something like this:

"Hello. I'm [author name], *and my novel,* A Time for Tea, *is an eighty-thousand-word cozy mystery about a blind librarian who solves crimes in her small Welsh village. It's similar in tone to* Murder by the Sea, *which I see from your website you represented. This is my first novel, although I've had mystery stories published in* [credits]."

This pitch shows the author has done their homework, and in many cases, the agent would want to hear more. The conversation might end with the agent asking for a partial manuscript, maybe the first fifty pages or so. I've seen this happen so many times at conferences, and the writer comes out of the session stunned, starry-eyed, and grinning from ear-to-ear. It's wonderful to see dreams come true, so give them the moment and don't harangue them with lectures about what other paths they might want to think about. If they're happy, let them live their dreams. Of course, if someone asks for your advice, wait a bit and then give them the truth as you see it. Just don't volunteer to be a buzzkill or dream-crusher, and remember that timing is everything.

Remember that you don't need anyone's permission to publish, nor do you have to wait years to be chosen by gatekeepers. You can publish independently *while* you pursue a traditional path if you want, becoming a hybrid author, or any way that makes you happy. And if you achieve outstanding success as an independent, the traditional publishers will then want you even more.

Dale T. Phillips

Editors- You DO Need Them

Editors are **essential** to improving your work and aiding your success. Most writers are blind to the faults in their own writing, despite being sharp about discovering them in every other printed work. I'm no exception, and though I'm paid to evaluate and edit other manuscripts, I still pay another good editor to help make *my* manuscripts better. However, when I send my manuscript to my editor, I've done a great deal of cleanup beforehand, to give her less work to do. Note that some editors charge by the page, which is a crap system. Something that needs a lot of cleanup takes far more time than a very clean page, so go for editors who work hourly, to save yourself money. And get honest ones- my editor thought the latter half of a novel needed rewriting, so sent it back for revisions before spending hours editing something that would be significantly changed.

There are different types of editors and editing, and disagreement about which is which, as some of these terms are variable. Some combine more than one of these in their inclusive editing. Know up front what you're getting and paying for.

• Manuscript evaluation/appraisal— This high-level check is for the essential quality of your manuscript.

Does it work as a book? Does it have commercial viability? Does it have the elements it needs for publication, or are there major problems which must be corrected first?

• Developmental or Story editing— This is a check that the structural story works as it is, or may need chapters/characters moved around, added/deleted, or simply further detail in certain areas. Completed story arcs?

• Line editing— This check is for content and flow, things like consistency of voice, point-of-view, tone, and clarity, and slack writing which may sag or need some punching up.

• Copy editing— This type drills down to the precision bits on a word-for-word basis, usually working to a style type or sheet. Different copyeditors work using different standards, though, so make sure you agree with yours.

• Proofreading— Checking for any and every error, in text, layout, numbering, placement, etc.

• Fact checking— If you have a manuscript with a lot of facts in it, you may need one of these editors for verification of the information you've included.

Because most Indie writers don't have a lot of surplus income, they blanch when told they MUST have a good editor for their work, before it goes out to the buying public. Since good editing runs from $25-50 or more per hour, they despair at not having hundreds of dollars to make their work better. Especially when they hear that there are different levels of editing, and the work might need more than one editing pass. *Ouch!* When you're talking about a thousand dollars or more for each book, that's real money to most writers.

And if the writer is expecting an editor to wear all those hats and correct all the errors in a manuscript in one pass, and to do it cheaply, well, that's like looking for unicorns. So the money-impaired writer is tempted to skip the process altogether, or to assume a publisher (if they go that route) will take care of that. Skipping (or even skimping) on editing is a bad business decision that will adversely affect a writing career. As a reader, when I encounter a poorly-edited book, I seldom read that author again. If their story wasn't even worth an editing pass, then it's not worth wasting my time to read it, or anything else by them. So what's a poor writer to do?

It's never too early to start your search for a good editor, to get them lined up for when you've got a work ready for their red pen. Know what type of editing you'll be getting for the money, and get some samples up front. Many writers got burned paying for poor levels of edits they didn't want or need. You'll need to do some careful research for this one, to find someone you're comfortable working with, who can be trusted to work in a timely fashion, and provides quality for the price. You can start an editing fund right away, even if it's a few bucks a week. Forego the pricey coffee, young hipster, and bank those four dollars so your work will be better. Your stories are worth it, aren't they?

Here are some ways to get your manuscript in shape BEFORE you send it to the editor. The less work the well-paid editor does, the less you pay. You'll see that each method described here will do some of the work of different editors. It'll catch a lot of simple stuff, but it's extra work that takes an editor more time to point out and mark up.

•   Study the information about feedback, using beta readers, writing groups, and workshops. Get advance feedback for your work through the methods described there. Story edits for flaws can cause massive rewrites, driving up the cost of your editing, and taking a lot of extra time. When your story passes muster with all your *free* feedback sources, *then* send it on to a pro.

•   Our brains play tricks when scanning text, gliding over mistakes, so copy the text into a different type of file, and change the font, and the size, and print it out. You'll catch a lot of things you didn't see before.

- Get a helper, someone to listen, and read through your work- slowly. Do this in stages, so you don't overdo it. Mistakes will sound like dull clunks in many cases. You'll wince when hearing some of the stuff you wrote that looked okay on paper. Mark it all, and fix that stuff!

- Some people recommend reading it backwards. If that floats your boat, go for it. Haven't tried that one yet.

Check with the editor in advance when you know you'll soon have a manuscript for them. They might be busy for weeks with the work of someone else, and you don't want to have your manuscript sitting around. Once you've put in all the free feedback, and had other eyes on the text, NOW you're ready for a proven, *paid* set of eyes for your work. You'll swear up and down your manuscript is perfect, but you'll be shocked to discover what you missed when you get it back.

On the path to success, *quality* is necessary to establish a trusted "brand"- with clean, well-told stories, your audience will grow. Having a lot of mistakes in your manuscript will get you dinged in reviews, and may convince some to not buy or read it. Lay the groundwork for a long-term writing career you can be proud of.

Feedback

As a writer, your work is *always* up for critique— I call it showing your homework for correction to the world. And it will be critiqued, so much better to have it ripped apart and made better *before* it's published, right? There are a number of ways to get valuable feedback before the work goes to an editor, and before it goes out to the world of readers.

A good critique writing group can give various levels of usable feedback. Even if they they're not perfect, they can catch a lot of stupid mistakes. For my first few novels, my local group was invaluable in finding the dumb stuff before the editors did. They bluntly told me when some passage of writing did not work for them. It wasn't pleasant to hear, but it was necessary. We always told people we'd give honest feedback, not just say nice things about all the work. A couple of writers came in and expected everyone to tell them how wonderful the piece was. When they heard the least little criticism, they strenuously objected. They didn't last long, and most likely never got published.

Many of these groups have a regular meeting schedule. Usually someone reads a section of their work (sent in advance, or read cold on the spot), and then the members of the group offer feedback on what they heard. Though the quality may vary, it's good to hear others read your work, because it makes you cognizant of how your own sounds. Reading your work aloud alerts you to things that don't sound quite right. And offering feedback to others makes you a better writer, as you have to think about the words and the story, and how they're presented.

When offering feedback, be constructive. Let them know when something works particularly well, and help them to make their own writing better. Many times you'll get feedback on your own writing that tells you something doesn't work. Usually they cannot specify exactly how to fix it, because that's up to you. Specifics are for the author, but if the same thing doesn't ring true for more than one person, they might be on to something. You may sometimes get feedback that's flat wrong, so always consider the source, and see if you can get confirmation from others. Advice from someone with a lot of publications may be more useful than a tip from someone with few or no publications.

Finding a Group

How does one find a feedback group?

• Check local libraries and bookstores to see if any already exist.

•   Check online for information about potential groups.

•   Check with writing organizations to see if they know of any in your area.

•   Go on social media to discover existing groups.

•   If you can't find a group in your area, you may be able to work with an online group.

•   You may have to start one, if there are none in your area.

The best feedback comes from workshopping— really intense editing by people who are writers and willing to share solid criticism with each other. For this, 3-4 people is about right. Best is when you're all at similar ability levels in your writing. Send out good chunks of work, 25 pages from each person, and meet once a month, with all the marked-up manuscript edits on all work in hand. Then drill down to the nitty-gritty, and discuss what works and what doesn't in the story, and possible fixes. At that rate, you can go through a good book length a year. You'll raise each other's' level as well, getting better at spotting bad writing, both in their work and your own.

Beta readers are those who've agreed to read your entire work in draft format, and give you feedback, one-on-one. For brutally honest feedback, don't ask friends—rather get someone who doesn't care about your good opinion. Friends will usually take pains not to hurt your feelings. And this person just has to be a reader, not necessarily a writer, and so much better if they understand the genre. You want them to tell you what didn't work in the book. Though some will read for nothing, many times the people work out a swap, each critiquing the work of the other. You can find people for this using the similar methods to finding a group. Use as many Beta readers as you like and are comfortable with.

Some people post their draft work online for public critique. Andy Weir's *The Martian* did this, with good results. I don't prefer this method, but there are sites who provide an opportunity for people who like this. If it works for you, go for it.

Reviews

After a work is published, the public starts in to tell the writer what they thought. Some writers choose not to read reviews for various reasons. If you get 99 good reviews, but one bad one, you might focus on the bad instead of accepting the good. With the whole world as potential critiquers, there will always be someone who doesn't like what you've written. Don't wind up second-guessing yourself because of one opinion by one reader. However, if a number of reviews point out similar things that didn't work for them, consider if their feedback has merit.

Reviews are harder to get for everyone these days, but especially for Indie writers. Many established venues don't review Indie-written books, although some of those are changing. You can now purchase a pricey review from *Kirkus* and *Publisher's Weekly*, if you think it's worth it. No guarantee if you'll get a good one or not, but if you've got money and want to gamble, hey, it's your funds. I have one data point from an Indie writer who got lucky and received a good review after going this route, and he says it helps when approaching libraries and bookstores, about the last people that read those industry publications.

While traditionally-published writers get almost automatic glowing reviews from their publishing-house mates, in a logrolling way, Amazon tends to remove posted reviews written by people with any provable (mostly via social media) connection to the Indie writer-who are the very people the Indies start getting reviews from!

Your best bet (again, more work!) is to research the many places that still review Indie books, and request one. Usually you'll send them a copy (electronic is best- no cost), and they have to acknowledge this fact when they review. I've had good success doing this, and received many great reviews I can use for promotion. Keep a list of where and when you send requests, and the results.

Sending print copies out for review is expensive (especially overseas), so make sure it's worth it. Many places accept ebook versions, and there are a growing number of places that review audio books- these are terrific, because most other type of book reviewers are busy many months ahead, but an audiobook might get reviewed much quicker.

Bad Reviews and Rejection

Always remember that no matter how good, there are some people in the world that will not like or appreciate what you have created. Ignore them, they do not matter. Many writers feel personally rejected when their *work* is rejected in some fashion, and their self-esteem suffers as a result. Dean Wesley Smith has a great post on this. Imagine getting five thousand rejections, as he did. That would sink many writers. He just kept going, and selling. For the win! The number of yesses is worth more than all the noes.

How to Be a Successful Indie Writer

With traditional publishing, writers were rejected most of the time. I still get stories turned down by some venues. When that happens, it quickly goes out to the next market, and so on, until it gets sold or put into a collection. By doing this, you tend not to focus on the rejection, but on getting it to the next person and making the sale. Back when rejections were sent by mail, I would save the printed form in a binder— and note when the magazine went out of business before I did. I finally stopped, because many of the stories were selling more often, and I didn't prefer to print out rejection emails. But it's a great reminder when you're down to look back at what someone didn't want, which sold somewhere else.

Dale T. Phillips

Making Your Plan

"The moment one definitely commits oneself, then providence moves too. All sorts of things occur to help one that would never otherwise have occurred. A whole stream of events issues from the decision, raising in one's favor all manner of unforeseen incidents, meetings and material assistance which no man could have dreamed would have come his way. Whatever you can do or dream you can, begin it. Boldness has genius, power and magic in it. Begin it now."

Sometimes attributed to Johann Wolfgang von Goethe (though it may be someone else's)

Since success is far more likely when you have a good plan and follow it, you'll want to work on this critical part a bit. Realize that the plan will likely change along the way, and that's okay, as various life events and opportunities arise, especially if you have schedules, which you should. The plan needs to be recorded in some format: I use basic office software spreadsheets. Writing down things makes them real, and sets it more firmly in your mind. Charting your progress keeps you focused and motivated. Do what works for you, and make it easily accessible, because you'll refer to this frequently, to keep following the plan.

The plan isn't hopes or simply *dreams*, it's achievable goals *that are within your power*. You can certainly write down your dreams, or incorporate them as part of a Vision Board, but your *plan* is doable steps to success. Winning awards, selling 100 thousand copies, being on Oprah, these are outside of your control. What is within your control is easy: what you'll produce, by when, and how you'll get it out to the world, and what other steps you'll take. All while you're learning more and creating your business. Work by work, win by win, you set each foundation stone to build that house of success.

Series

Series are a great way to get more books out quicker, as you don't have to rebuild the novel world each time. They're more likely to get you repeat readers and build your fan base. One writer I know is a smart cookie who has all the keywords and ad campaigns down, knows some of how to market, but all five of his novels are in different genres with no connection. A reader finds one of his books they enjoy, but nothing else like it by the same author, so sales are one-offs. That's why the books don't sell, but he doesn't do anything about it, except gripe about how they're not selling. So he's discouraged and wants to give up. People buy my entire mystery series, because when they find a fictional world they like, they enjoy returning to it again and again. Remember, there are many series which survived past the demise of their creator, because people enjoy those worlds, even when written by others. One reason why fanfic is so popular.

Stories

If you can add stories and collections to your output, that gets you to success quicker. Each story publication is another showcase ad for you when it comes out, as well as a chance for more promotion (and some form of payment). They can be finished and published quicker than novels, and serve as good credit-building. They get you through the long haul between books, and keep you going, a refreshing change of pace from the long grind of a novel. If you get a story into an anthology or collection with other writers, there are good connections to make. Having a book of your stories is a good resume addition, and an inexpensive way for new readers to find you. More in the store!

Start with making a goal of writing one story a month. At that pace, you've got enough in a year and a half to Indie publish a couple of collections. That lets you easily get into the publishing process, and puts some product up, apart from one novel or two. It helps to get the ball rolling. Momentum is nice to have. It's good to keep a list of ideas and titles for future works, be they novels, stories, or whatever. If I need an idea for a targeted anthology story or get stuck on what to write, I look at the ideas and titles I've recorded to see if anything sparks me to begin on that. So I always have material to write.

For the master plan, break it down into large segments. First, what you expect to have done by a year from the start date. You can do a lot in a year, more than you think. Second, what you'll have done three years from now. That gives you enough time to put out some quality work that will get you noticed. Then a future date, by which you'll have done enough to be successful. Say five to seven years, by which you'll enough good novels written and published, and a lot of stories. More than many writers.

Then detail each time segment in your plan, making milestones and goals. First year, first book. Say fifty thousand words, a short novel, only one thousand words a week. When you get to five thousand words, that's a major milestone— your first ten percent! Hitting these milestones makes you feel like you're really progressing, and keeps the momentum. As studies show, setting specific intentions greatly increase your chances of success.

Then the other details— how will the book be edited: critique group, beta readers, editor? Have you started on those parts yet? If not, set a period of time to research, and put that in the schedule. If you haven't done it, it may be difficult to estimate, but it's good to rough out some sort of time frame, even if preliminary. Remember, you can adjust the plan later as more information becomes available. Set a reasonable time for editing, especially if this is an early novel, which may require some restructuring and story work. One of the great aspects of the Indie world is that you don't have to publish a book until it's ready. There have been a number of occasions where I wanted a book done by a certain date, but it needed more work, so it got delayed. Don't publish until it's good, but don't spend eternity on it, either. Get work out rather than let it sit for too many years unpublished.

Publishing

Apart from editing, do you know how to publish? Print, ebook, audiobook? Do you have a cover artist, and know how to format? Do you know what platforms you'll distribute on? Do you have all your marketing materials planned out? Do you know the other aspects of what comes after? If not, set periods for research. Ebooks can be published quickly, as soon as they're ready. Print needs more formatting, and time to order a proof copy to verify it looks like it's supposed to. Audiobooks need to be produced, and take the longest time. Adjust plans accordingly, and if you don't know, just put a guesstimate or TBD (To Be Determined) in the time frame for now.

Definitely set the schedule for learning, and not just the publishing knowledge you'll need. Can you absorb a new craft book on writing every 3-4 months? That gives you a few every year, and helps you improve much quicker. Plan on a course, online or in-person event every year, on some aspect of your writing that needs improvement. For that, I recommend at least one live writer conference a year, where you can learn a great deal in a few days. Budget for it, because they're invaluable in advancing your writing career and making connections with other writers and fans.

And that's just the start. See what I mean about how most people don't get that far? It's daunting to think about all you have to know, in addition to the writing. It took me about two years to learn enough of what I needed to publish my own books and break out as full Indie. Then I just took off and didn't look back, though I'm still always learning. It does get easier as time goes by, because once you've acquired certain knowledge, you don't have to relearn it.

Getting There

By following a good plan, in three years, you can be set on your success path quite readily. You've got some good books published, maybe some other material as well, you have your marketing material all prepared, you know how to contact libraries and bookstores, you've learned a lot. You've learned how to take feedback and have some trusted advance readers who will help. You've got some reviews and been interviewed a few places. After you get many of the preliminaries out of the way, plan to step up your production. Since you need less research time, put it into making your books awesome.

And the next few years after that should determine how well you'll do. If you're always moving forward, making plans and achieving goals, producing good work, you'll be surprised at how much you can accomplish.

My original plan was to get a good start on success with ten good novels, ten story collections, and one hundred published stories. If I can keep writing, I should reach that goal by next year, ten years in.

And that's just the beginning!

In a famous Harvard study of goal-setting, a class was asked the following:

"Have you set clear, written goals for your future and made plans to accomplish them?"

- 3% said Yes

- 13% had goals, but not written down

- 84% had no specific goals at all.

Ten years later, the 13% with unwritten goals earned *double* the 84% with no goals.

The 3% with written goals earned *10 times all the rest put together.*

Dale T. Phillips

Productivity

"Writing a novel is like driving at night with your headlights on—you can only see a little of the road ahead, but you can make the whole journey that way."

—E.L. Doctorow

You write a novel the way you'd eat an elephant—one small bite at a time.

Writing even *one* novel is a lot of damned hard work. *Continuing* to write them is little short of obsessive. But to be successful, you'll have to keep doing it over and over. Unlike singers, however, you get to do different ones each time, not the same thing over and over.

Every writer has a different way of doing the work. Two major types are as follows (with many of us doing one or the other, or both, at times):

• *Plotters*, who carefully detail everything before writing, doing the outline and seeing the scene first.

• *Pantsers*, who write "by the seat of their pants," just jumping in without a complete structure in advance.

Dean Wesley Smith uses this method, which he calls "Writing into the Dark." He has an advantage, though, in having done it several hundred times!

The best way to be productive is to write every day if you can, not to wait for inspiration. That's an excellent method, because it *builds the habit*. If you can do that, absolutely it's a wonderful way to be productive. Me, I do it the "wrong" way (even though fellow writers compliment me on my productivity, which I find amusing). I have to be inspired by the ancient Greek concept of The Muse, which many say is not effective, because you won't write as much. Lucky for me, I take The Muse seriously, and She often drops by to tell me what to write next. Which sometimes messes me up, because I shift projects at a moment's notice.

For too long, I was working on three different novels, and not completing any. One was 75% done, one was 50% done, and one was 25% done. Which all adds up to *zero* percent finished. There were some publishing strategy changes, and various issues in the narratives which bogged me down.

Then I finished one novel, but before I got to the other two, another novel sprang into being. I wrote most of that, and got stuck again when illness, depression, and the New World of Covid-plague hit, in rapid succession. I was down and out for too long a time, before I decided that writing would give me back my life. Indeed it did, and I burst forth with a completed and published novel, a new story, a finished draft of another novel. Before completing the next novel, though (my plan), *this* book demanded to be written and published. And there's so much to cover that it just keeps growing. No matter. I do not argue with The Muse, who has been kind to me in my pursuit of success.

Write whenever you want, or can: early morning, late at night, on lunch breaks, whatever. Find the time that works best for you. Short stretches or long marathon sessions, doesn't matter. Keep a notebook handy for ideas that come to you when you're doing other things like driving or showering or taking a walk (when many ideas turn up).

If you have trouble, try the **Pomodoro Method**, of sprints and movement. http://graemeshimmin.com/the-pomodoro-technique-for-writers/

One good habit is to set aside your writing time as the primary task. Writers procrastinate better than anyone else, and it's so easy to get sidetracked into little things that writing time can easily slip away. Write first, do all else later. Don't do research in your writing time, because it's easy (and lots of fun) to fall down the rabbit hole. If you come to a passage that needs to be researched, just mark it as such and move on.

Doing the Math

If you're just starting out, you may produce at a slower rate. That's okay, it will just take you longer. If you're going to be a *successful* Indie writer, you'll need a fair amount of good work. Do you know how long on average it takes you do finish, edit, and publish each book? If not, start with an estimation of writing one book a year, 50-100,000 words. When you get more experienced, you'll definitely want to increase this output, but it's a good place to begin. At that pace, it will take you roughly five years to write five good books, which will (simply by that output) put you in the top 20% of all published writers.

Have you got at least five good books in you, just as a start?

So- your first novel. Say 75,000 words, and you want it done in a year. That's only 1500 words a week (a few hundred a day), around 5 pages. Fifty weeks later, you've got 250-plus pages, and those 75,000 words. Congratulations- you've done more than many who set out to do this. It may not be the best yet, but you got it done. If you learn to play an instrument, you hit some bad notes while doing so.

Celebrate!

Then get to work on the second novel. You've practiced for a year, so maybe this one will go faster. Up your word count to 2500 words a week. Still quite doable. This means you'll get this one done in just over six months. How about that? Almost half the time. And you learned a lot more. And it's probably better than book one.

Celebrate!

Write the third book, slightly better pace. Finish.

Celebrate!

Two years total, three books under your belt.

Starting to get the hang of it? Hopefully. Rinse and repeat.

If you need a million words to get really good, how many can you write in a year? A book a year is a decent pace, better than most, but for more success, you might want to step it up some. If you can put out 5,000 words a week, you can have 250,000 in a year, and a million words in only four years.

How to Be a Successful Indie Writer

One book a year might net you a few hundred dollars in income (or a few thousand), but you want more, you want volume. The more you write and publish, the more you'll make. If you want to make 48,000 dollars a year, you'll need 4,000 dollars a month, or roughly two thousand total sales at two dollars profit each, or 500 sales a week. One book will sell x number of copies, ten books will sell much more. So you want to get to ten good books published, as quickly as possible. That takes discipline and dedication.

Figure out how much you make per hour, and scale up. If you make a penny a word, an hour of good writing at one thousand words nets you roughly ten dollars. That's your scale. If you want to make 48,000 dollars a year, you have to write faster, or get paid more. Daunting, yes.

So strive for that Long Tail, and eventual discoverability of all your work. After six to ten books, you should be selling more of everything. Each new book adds to the total. The '*Halo effect*' means that other works are bought because people discovered one or more of your works. Especially if you have a series, or connected books.

In the old way of publishing, some authors could get by with one book a year. Today, you'll likely have to be more productive to make a decent income. So it's up to you to determine your level of success.

Dean Wesley Smith calls his copyright and production output **The Magic Bakery**.

https://www.amazon.com/Magic-Bakery-Copyright-Fiction-Publishing-ebook/dp/B074D7K3ZD/ref=sr_1_1?dchild=1&keywords=the+magic+bakery&qid=1599945073&s=books&sr=1-1

Imagine that you have a storefront, with all your items for sale within. If you have one book in one format, you have one product. Ever walk into a store with a single product? You likely won't stay long. For you as a successful author, you want variety and choice, different price points, and for shoppers to come back again and again to buy more. A series can bring them back for more. Put your work out as ebook, as print, as audio, whatever other formats may happen, such as graphic novels. The other aspect of *The Magic Bakery* is that as an Indie, you can keep licensing pieces of each product, while keeping the original. Traditional publishing buys the whole product, which you then cannot resell. But Dean made thousands of dollars from one story, by licensing different pieces of it. Make your work into a virtual storefront, and fill it with tempting merchandise.

It's amusing to me that when I set up my display at book events, people look at the output, and think I'm prolific as hell, when I feel like a slacker who doesn't do enough. I smile and say, *"If you want it badly enough, you'll work for it."* I sell more than most writers at these events, because of my variety, and the different price points (with prices shown for each book, so browsers don't have to ask). A few secrets of my success. I point out that someone can grab a book of short stories for little more than a cup of coffee, or get a good novel for half the price of a hardcover in a bookstore. And because people love a bargain, I'll give them a price break if they want to buy more than one book. By having so much available, with ebooks and audio of everything, I'll offer them other free versions of the work when they purchase print (which costs me nothing). People remember, and come back in subsequent years to buy more. And every year they come back, there's more to sell.

Advantage, productivity.

Idea Mines

It's good to keep files of ideas, titles, character sketches, turn of phrase. When you need a new idea, scan these files for things that spark your imagination. I've got hundreds of potential titles in one file, and ideas for new tales in another. I'll never run out of things to write.

Chart Your Success

Because our minds gloss over the day-to-day, the usual and familiar, it's quite useful to keep a writing log for recording what steps you take and see how much you can do over time. Writing a book may seem like it goes on forever, so keep logs of what you do, to keep on track and keep motivated.

This can be as simple as making a time and word count entry in a notebook, or in a spreadsheet or document on a computer. You want to build momentum, so that a string of days of writing encourages you to do more. Each day that you've put new words down is a success! It's great to look at the accumulated results after a few months of work, and it truly feels like accomplishment.

You should also keep track of other parts of writing activities and successes. Publications, new editions, acceptances, good reviews, big sales, milestones reached, all that and more come together into a success chart. Record what advances you've made, and they will mount up into a tidal wave. You want to look back and see that you've made progress. Little steps in the right direction for big results.

Professionalism

Writing is like music- if you only practice at home, and don't perform in public, how will you make money at it?

Getting Paid

Stephen King always said that if you write something which someone pays you for, and you then pay the light bill with that money, that makes you a professional. I always liked that framing. And you should get good enough that you are always compensated for your writing. Often, people ask writers for written pieces for free, saying "You'll get good exposure." But, as the old saying goes, *You can die of exposure...*

There's a great Harlan Ellison rant you can find on the Internet (*Pay the Writer*), since he ran into so many folks who wanted free work or promotion from him. People who wouldn't dream of asking a plumber to come out and fix their sink for free will think nothing of asking for a story or a writer's time for no compensation. Very often, the world does not value the time or effort of a writer (or other creative artists). Your job as a professional is to make them understand that your time and work has value.

Dale T. Phillips

Wil Wheaton has a good take on this as well:

http://wilwheaton.net/2015/10/you-cant-pay-your-rent-with-the-unique-platform-and-reach-our-site-provides/

Of course, there are exceptions. When you're starting out, you may do a few pieces for no money just to accumulate publishing credits, if you don't have enough other ones. Some people publish anthologies to support a charity, and they'll ask you to contribute a story, and I've certainly done some of these. But most of the time, resist working for free. If you don't value your work, who else will?

The great thing about Indie publishing is that you usually get paid much quicker than with traditional publishing. Distribution sites pay in a timely fashion, while waiting for royalties from traditional publishers can take years. A number of independent, realistic polls and studies have provided reports on who makes what, and the results are eye-opening. On average, for an author debuting in the last few years, the average numbers for earnings were heavily in favor of Indie writers.

Demeanor

Acting at all times as a professional, be aware that your public persona is always on display, and is an essential part of your brand. Don't be a slob at public events. If you rant in person or on social media, or get involved in social media squabbles, you can do irreparable harm to your career. I've stopped reading even talented writers who exposed themselves as absolute intolerant bigots (or worse). If you act like a jerk at events or online, people won't want to deal with you or read your works. If you promise things and don't deliver, you'll quickly get a reputation as unreliable, and people won't want to work with you. If you create and publish sloppy work, people will rightly mark you as an amateur, not a professional. Treat everyone with respect, and act with integrity.

Don't whine, vent, or overshare in public (too many writers do this). Don't go to a conference and engage in bad behavior, such as getting publicly drunk, hitting on people, hitting people— this happens a lot with some, and they do not get invited back. Don't get into a literary feud, publicly trashing other writers, in reviews or otherwise. Don't be the backbiting jerk. The Golden Rule applies, so don't do or say anything to someone you wouldn't want them to do or say to you.

And DO NOT reply to bad reviews. Just don't. When you roll around with a skunk, you're both going to stink. It will do you no good, and make you look completely unprofessional. They happen, and sure, they're probably wrong. But learn to ignore them, and focus on the good ones you have.

Helping Others

An old saying goes *"be nice to people on your way up, because you'll meet them later on your way down."* I always enjoy helping other writers, because I know how tough this game is, and how a kind word or helping hand can make things so much better. Be the type of writer people want to help, as many love to give back— but don't do it just for expectation of return. If it's for any type of "writers helping others" charity (bookstores, libraries, or cause), I almost always contribute something when asked.

Help can come in many forms: reviews, advice, assistance, sharing information, working together for a common goal. Don't overextend yourself, though, or take too much time from your writing. For example, I still have a day job, so I cannot volunteer for long-term positions or tasks in the many writer organizations I work with. Instead, I help with good ideas and do one-offs, events or tasks which can be completed in a short time, so I can get back to my writing.

Many, many people have helped me in my writing career. I've been very fortunate, and strive to pass that along to others. For me, success is a two-way street, where I do better when other writers do better. The best part I've found about being Indie is that we tend to help each other much more than traditional publishing writers— we're co-operators, not competitors. For example, I host interviews with other writers on my website, giving them free promotion to help sell more books.

Always be Learning

Continue to polish your craft with books, articles, workshops, seminars, panels. When you take a class, it's always good to know if the person giving it is truly qualified. Check out their credentials and books beforehand. Does it look like they know what they're doing? Are they reasonably successful at it? Get your questions ready before the course begins, and learn as much as you can.

Tools

As an Indie writer, you'll need a lot of tools, much more so than traditionally-published writers. Mostly because you'll be doing the work they leave to others: both to ensure it's done well, correctly, and timely, and to save yourself a great deal of money. You don't need to know them all at once, you'll learn pieces of things as time goes by. We'll cover some of the best items to have in your Indie writer toolkit. Though all you really need to start writing is paper and a pen or pencil, you'll eventually go for more. So you go Old School and use a typewriter (I had to, for years), recorded audio to be transcribed later (if you want to really be different), or you learn to use a computer to commit your words to a file you can send electronically.

It would be almost impossible these days to be successful as an Indie writer without some form of computer or screen for all one must do, unless someone else does it all for you. There are a variety of word-processing applications available, so use whatever works for you. Submitting your work elsewhere requires files be in standard formats, so Microsoft Word is the most common software in use. Just realize that we cannot go into the pros and cons of every potential tool here, so you'll have to do your research on what might work for you.

Many computer *desktop publishing* tools make your job easier and faster, for setup, spelling, grammar, formatting, saving and sending files, etc. Some tools are free, and some cost money. *Always research before spending.* Will you really learn and use this software so much that it's worth it for the price? Does anyone you know have a copy you can work with? How about your local library: they sometimes have licenses for certain applications. If not, maybe you can get a demo version from the company, for a 30-day evaluation. Or there are sometimes reduced-price student versions.

Here are some of the common ones. I'll probably leave out someone's favorite, so if you've found any that have been useful, send the info along, and I'll work it into future updates.

File Types for print and ebooks:

- PDF

- Text (.txt)

- (Kindle and others) .mobi

- (Barnes and Noble Nook and others) .epub

Formatting:

- Vellum

- InDesign

Covers:

- Canva

- Illustrator

- PhotoShop

- Powerpoint- I'm told it's possible to produce covers using this.

Email List management:

- Mailchimp

Other:

- Backups- many writers have lost work to computer crashes, so use something that backs up frequently. We've used Carbonite, and it's been very useful for restoring files.

- Scribe- useful for organizing a book.

• Keywords- Publisher (KDP) Rocket. Helps you find the right tags to put your book higher up in searches for books of that type.

• BookFunnel- An author service that specializes in ebook and audio distribution, sending ARCs, and creating tools that save time and sanity.

• Website design, blogs, and hosting- many. Wordpress is free, but there's many others.

Part Three

Setting Up the Business

Dale T. Phillips

It's a Business

Disclaimer: As always, seek professional advice from licensed and qualified experts before entering into any legal matter.

As an Indie working for success, you are a small business, and will need to adopt some attitudes of a business mentality. I'd never planned on this aspect when I set out to write, but it's really necessary for any kind of long-term career. Most writers don't know how to start or run a business. As with other parts of this book, there are numerous resources to guide you in thinking about this and setting it up: read some books, take some courses, talk to professionals. The Small Business Association has resources for helping, and your local community might have more. Help is available to educate yourself.

The reason for having a business are many, but the most important is to make money, to take in more than you spend. You'll be forking over sums to license artwork, create works, put them up for sale, and market them, and you want the return profits of sales of those works. A business is a formal way of tracking the money flow in and out. It provides tax advantages, and also helps you to think like a professional instead of a hobbyist.

When I decided to go independent of other publishers, I knew it was time to create my own small-press publishing company, to have that "company imprint" upon the books. Having a publishing imprint upon your books is a way to indicate your more advanced level of seriousness.

A company? But how? You don't need an LLC or anything complicated. In my state, there's a cheap and easy way, called a *"Doing Business As"* (DBA). It's the shorthand way of creating a company with a name (don't make it your own personal name) to do business under. Now you have a front company, and can keep all writing costs separate from your non-writing life— and taxes. To create a DBA, you need a company name (we chose a unique name that won't get tangled on Internet searches with other companies), a bank account in that name, and you need to file papers to register with your town clerk. Where we live, it's only $40 for every four years.

Once you have the DBA company set up, you'll want a website and a company logo, which will be the image that represents the company, and which will go on all your published books. For tax purposes, you can apply for a Tax Identification Number (TIN) for the business, which you can use for your business, instead of having your personal Social Security number exposed more often.

That's most of what you need to start. You'll need to keep some sort of record-keeping for taxes, with different places for costs, mileage, inventory, income, etc. A big plus is that as a business, you do get some tax breaks for the business costs you spend, so you'll want to consult with a competent accountant at some point. You'll need to think about sales tax. If you make enough, you may have to file taxes quarterly.

Many writers are incredibly naïve about business, about the value of their work, and about how much most services are worth. Add to that the desperation of some to see their name in print at any cost, and it's a recipe for being taken. Anytime there is money involved, there are predators who will take advantage of others, and the publishing business has many willing to do so: book doctors, book designers, formatters, publishing assists, marketers, publicists, any aspect of the business has some people charging too much for sub-par services. Before you hire anyone for any aspect of publishing, vet them thoroughly! Educate yourself, or you'll learn the hard and expensive way. Know the costs of services, and what you'll get for your money.

And speaking of money, you'll need to think about this for book events where you can sell your own copies. Do you need to consider sales tax at this venue? Will you accept checks? Not everyone carries cash anymore. For credit cards, you'll want some commercial application, such as *Square*, which allows you to take credit card payments easily. To pay and get paid electronically, you'll want another commercial application for that, such as *PayPal* or *Venmo*. Find easy ways to deal with handling money, so it doesn't become a problem.

Now that you have a publishing company, do you want to deal with other writers? I don't, because it's such a hassle, too complex and time consuming, and I have so much of my own work I don't even have time to complete. But if you own a publishing company, you may have opportunities to do so. Think long and hard before you decide on this, and if you go forward, get qualified advice, and always have contracts in place to spell out everything.

Because it's such an up-and-down business, you might have a good year or two followed by several lean ones, or vice-versa. For example, few saw this current plague coming, and it completely changed the bookselling landscape overnight. All plans went out the window, and writers are scrambling to figure out how to keep going in a world gone insane and deadly.

This is another great reason you need to use a business model, to budget money wisely. Any windfall can disappear over time or through in unwise spending, and you're stuck without the money for necessities. Cover the bottom line first, then set aside any extra for unforeseen future happenings.

So make a business plan, much of which just a big To-Do list. Set your goals in timeframes, such as yearly quarters, like other businesses do. Make yearly folders. You don't have to fill them in yet, just plan for later. Nothing is set in stone. I constantly revise my plans, based on what pops up, via writing from the Muse or opportunities, like getting a batch of story rights reverted- suddenly I had a new collection I could put out! The whole schedule had to adjust.

Estate Management

Many writers have their works hit pay dirt after they've passed on. Thanks be to the copyright laws, your heirs can profit from your intellectual property long after you're gone. Make sure you have a letter of Final Instruction and a clear Will that states your intentions of who gets what, how your estate will be divided. Too many times there are ridiculous and expensive court battles because this was not done properly. If you have set up your company, who is going to own it, to run it? Or does it die with you? But it has valued assets, and payments could go on for years, so think it over.

Another thing you'll want to set up is a Literary Executor, someone you trust implicitly who will manage your output properly. It's going to have to be someone who understands the publishing business. Do you want others making new adaptations from your works? Finishing your incomplete books? Publishing your letters and drafts and notes? Some writers have asked for things to be destroyed after their death, and they weren't, and some have had invaluable work burned that shouldn't have been. Decide what you want preserved and what should never be seen. Remember, Edgar Allen Poe was unlucky enough to have an enemy decide what to do with his work after Poe died.

For more information, see the section *After You're Gone-Your Estate.*

Part Four

Setting Up the Book

Dale T. Phillips

Parts of a Book

Books today contain more than just the story. You'll want to do some research on all the front and back matter that are included with books, and are different for print versus ebooks. Placement of these for maximum effect is worth knowing. Here's a few things that are sometimes included (you don't always need them all):

Front Matter

• Title page— Always a right-hand page, this is the start. It lists your title in large font, centered both vertically and horizontally on the page. Below it goes your name (or your pen name). The publishing company's name and logo goes below.

• Copyright/Colophon page— List the copyright information, ISBN (only needed for print), legal disclaimers, and any information about contributors, such as cover artist or illustrator.

• Dedication— Usually appears on a right-hand page, about a third of the way down the page. You can dedicate to anything: people, groups, ideas.

• Epigraph/Quote— This can be a quote, song lyric, or statement that is the theme of the book or comments on the contents.

• Table of contents (Optional for fiction)— Helps more for navigation in ebooks, not needed for print, unless you want to name chapters to add to the commentary. If you use KDP or Barnes & Noble's built-in Nook publishing, the chapters might be automatically linked, depending on how you formatted the source files.

• Foreword/Preface/Introduction— Anything which serves as an introduction to a book, talking about its subject, scope, or aims. Or a commentary from the author, or one by another author.

• More by This Author— I include this in both the front and back of my books. Include any book you've written, whether or not it's the same genre, because people who like your writing probably want more. Cross-sell at every opportunity.

  • For a series, list in chronological or reverse chronological in order.

  • For an ebook, make these titles link directly to a sales page. Make it easy to find and buy your work.

Back Matter

• Appendices— Extra information like references, notes, or bibliographies. You'll see some at the end of this book.

- Author Notes— Anything extra you'd like to say about the book.

- Afterword/ About this Book — Another chance to say something extra. Can be about the book, the author, or whatever you want.

- About the author— This is for short, interesting biographical notes. Include your contact information for social media. For ebooks, make these into links.

- Acknowledgments— Thank the people who helped this book into creation. Can include editors, cover designer, Beta readers, even family, close friends, inspirations.

- Call to Action— Encourage the reader for more connection, such as signing up for your newsletter, connecting on social media, giving feedback. If the reader takes an extra step, they'll likely become a bigger fan, with more sales in the future.

- Connect with the Author— Give your readers a way to connect with you: email, website, social media, you want fans to connect.

- Sample of another one of your works— This is a teaser for the reader to check out more of your work, especially if they really liked the one they're reading. At every opportunity, you want your readers coming back for more.

Dale T. Phillips

Covers

"You can't judge a book by its cover."

Old Saying that's misleading, because many readers do

You cover is *vital* to the success of your book, because readers scan quickly, and take more time to check out books with covers they like. Your tiny thumbnail image will be up on the Internet against thousands of others, so make it eye-catching. A lousy cover usually indicates inferior inside material, and many readers won't bother. A great cover is a promise of better content inside. Many, many authors fail in this category, and their sales suffer as a result. The cover is the first indication of whether you're a professional or not, and may be the *only* chance you get of someone taking a look. To understand what good covers look like, check out the top best-sellers in a genre, and see what they have in common. Some websites show examples of bad covers, so check those out so you'll know what to avoid.

Traditional publishers boast of their packaging superiority, because Indie books have lousy covers, and for many, that's true— as it is with many of the traditional publishing covers. Or they'll just use stock images over and over. One traditional writer asked a fellow writer if she liked his latest cover— and it was almost exactly the one that had been on *her* previous book- from the same publisher! Barry Eisler, a best-selling top-notch writer, was stuck with the most unexciting, dumb-looking, green garage door for his *thriller* (an absolute sales-killer), and when he protested, the publisher would do nothing to remedy the situation. He soon left that publisher, costing them millions for a bad decision.

Trade-copy paperbacks are inexpensive to publish, but hardcovers may not be worth it for most Indie writers. They're expensive to produce, so unless you want a special edition, have legions of fans, or have a lot of extra money to burn, you may not want to bother. Few people will pay a lot for a pricey book by someone who's not famous or pushed by a big traditional publisher. Full color print books are also expensive, and harder to create, but if you've got a pet project that requires it, you'll want to spend some time planning it out.

If you cannot learn do the cover yourself (most writers cannot, as we work with words, not images) you may have to hire someone. This can get expensive, so you'll need to carefully spend time researching costs and quality. Yes, you can get the cheap designers, but you'll want to make sure to get something that works. Many writers who spent far too much on their covers (some thousands of dollars), got bad covers that still could have been done at a tenth of the cost. Now there are cover templates which can be had for bargain rates, and there are sites to inexpensively pay for cover art you can license to use commercially.

Some authors run A/B testing on prospective covers to see what people prefer, via their blog, website, or social media. If a number of people are strongly in favor one cover over another, the more popular is usually the one chosen by the author as a final.

First and foremost, the cover should reflect the genre and match your target audience, so that at a glance, people can guess what the book represents: horror book covers show darkness and spooky things, romance often shows two embracing people (usually with rumpled clothes), high fantasy shows someone in armor with a bladed weapon (and often a monster), Westerns show someone in a cowboy hat on a horse. You get the idea. So know the conventions of your genre, and do something that represents your content. If you don't know, look at several dozen top-selling books in the genre you wrote in.

Second, the title and the author name should be in easily readable fonts, with the proper size and color. Many get this wrong. If you look at a thumbnail (or a full-size cover from ten feet away) and cannot discern the title or author name clearly, it doesn't work. It may be the spacing, placement, size, background color, or font that are off, or a combination of those. Some use fonts that are just wrong, either unreadable as is or wrong for the genre. Again, examine other covers that work to see how they do it, and do something similar.

For full print covers, the spine and back cover need to be done properly. The title and author name should again be easy to read on the spine, and placed and spaced well. For the back, it takes some time to figure out the design and where things should go. You'll want some of the following:

•   Description/Tagline: a few exciting lines about the story inside that make a reader want to check it out.

•   Blurb (optional): a recommendation from some other writer (or reader) that praises your work.

•   Another work (optional): Sometimes you'll have an image and short description of another one of your other books here (especially for another volume in the series).

• Short Bio (optional): Some writers put these on the cover, though I prefer them in the book interior, at the back of the book. Unless you've got something so spectacular, like you were a spy, or astronaut, that will help sell the work on that information alone.

• Price, ISBN, and barcode: Whoever prints your book will likely request you to set aside an area to include a barcode, unless you have it set it up already. Again, compare your design with that of other successful book cover backs, and do what they do. Do you want to print your price on the cover? What about the ISBN, or will you have that just in the interior?

Once you've set your book up for print, you'll want a proof copy to look over before authorizing it to be published. If you publish through a site such as Amazon, you can request a single physical copy that you should carefully go through. Verify that the cover is eye-catching and professional, and the interior is done properly. Then have another careful set of eyes look it over.

The key is that your book should at a glance look like other quality books, because readers don't prefer ugly or amateur. At one book signing, my friend was launching his latest novel. Another writer asked about Indie versus Traditional. I said "let's compare," and put one of mine next to the one that was launching via a publisher. Same size, good covers, all was as it should be (and similar), the price was identical, and the interiors looked properly done. He said he couldn't see a difference, and that's the secret— except my friend would make a dollar for each one he sold, and my similar book would make ten dollars profit for each one I'd sold.

Advantage, Indie!

For a series, the branding should match on the covers. Go with a theme that makes them look like they belong together, for quick identification. Check out other author series to see what they have done.

Dale T. Phillips

Pricing

As an Indie, you get to set your own prices for your
books. Do some further research on this, as there are
articles and book chapters you'll want to refer to.
There's a lot of info on sweet spots for pricing. Just
look online, for example, and see what prices are for
book similar to yours. Ebooks sell the most at $3-5,
printed novels between $10-16. I don't price higher
than that, because fewer people will pay more for an
untried product, but at that level, they'll give it a try.
Some charts show that ebooks sell the most if they're
not over 4.99, so I'm running a sale on the pricier ones
to see if there's any movement. We Indies always get to
experiment!

Traditional publishers jack up the prices on their books,
both in print and ebook, because they have to pay
larger staffs. For print, I'm certainly not going to shell
out $30 or more for a hardcover, and for an ebook,
many readers don't want to pay $15 for one ebook
(myself included), when they can get three or more
quality ones for that price. For myself, I prefer to keep
prices low, so I can sell more, but still make a profit. At
a live show, I can even cut a deal if they buy more than
one book. The series novels are all priced the same, and
at a level so I can give a bookstore their 40% or more
and still make a profit. If I hand-sell one at full price, I

make about $10 net, so if anyone starts to balk on purchasing, I can give them a discount. People love a bargain, especially if you drop the price right then.

Print costs you money, but ebooks cost you little to nothing. If someone buys a print copy from me, I'll often offer the ebook for free as an extra bonus that's usually appreciated.

I aim for a price appropriate to what I'm selling, as follows:

- A short story collection (five tales): print, 4.99 (net about a dollar), ebook 2.99 (net almost $2). For perspective, I tell them they can have a book for the price of a coffee.
- Longer collections: ten tales- print 7.99, ebook 3.99, 30 tales- print 11.99, ebook 7.99
- Standalone short novels: print 9.99, ebook 3.99
- Series novels: print 15.99, ebook 4.99. Except the first series book, at 2.99. I want to get them hooked on the series, so I offer the first at a low bargain price.

Formatting

Note: This section is brief, because there are whole books on the subject, which give the granular level of detail you'll want. The Resources Appendix lists sources that will help, and all the book distributors have information available on their websites. Here we discuss text only. If you include images in your book, you will need additional learning or assistance. Here, formatting is essentially how a book is laid out and appears in a manuscript. It includes font, interior design, page layout, overall manuscript look, file types, and more. Don't freak out if this is too much. There is help available.

Badly formatted books will not sell and will net you terrible reviews. While ebooks are simple to format and produce, the layout of print books is more complicated and takes some skill and practice. Luckily there are great templates available, which makes your job much easier.

As always, if you find yourself unwilling to learn this part, you can pay someone else to do it. It doesn't cost much, but if you'll be producing a number of books, you may eventually want to save the repeated cost of paying for something you can do yourself for free.

For my layout formatting, I go quick and easy with a basic Microsoft Word file (.doc file), which is currently accepted by most (if not all) book distributors. I set up my template types for the different distributors, and for each book, just copy text into these renamed templates. There's one for Kindle only, one for Smashwords (all other ebook types), and one for print. For an ebook, it doesn't take long to set up once I have the text to put in it. Use standard fonts and verify what is recommended for the type of book you're producing. As for front and back matter, check out some of the thoughts of the formatting articles and books on placement and type. They'll tell you what to include and what to leave out, and where things should go. Of course, you'll also want to check out other books to see how it's done.

For print books, you can go upscale if you like clean, professional design. If you use a Mac, many people recommend Vellum, an application which is easy to learn and use. Further up the scale is InDesign, a tool of professional printers and formatters, but pricier, and much harder to learn.

Amazon has the option for a browser to "Look inside" and see how the interior and contents are displayed, and this is great. I use it when deciding on a book purchase. Sites like Smashwords allow you to set a percentage of the book the browser can read for free when you're setting the book up for publication. I usually select 15%.

ISBNs

An ISBN is an ID that one company sells (which is a monopoly), and a complete ripoff. My take on ISBN numbers is that they're a complete scam. If they were inexpensive, few would mind, but they charge big bucks, hundreds of dollars, for anybody buying a few, while traditional publishing companies can buy hundreds for very little unit cost.

https://www.myidentifiers.com/identify-protect-your-book/isbn/buy-isbn

After all, Canada gives ISBNs out for *free*, and Amazon gives you an ASIN number, a similar tracking number, for free. So why do Indies in this country get penalized for high prices for smaller amounts?

An ISBN allows companies to track and order print books, so although ebooks and audiobooks don't need them, it's a good idea to have them for your print version. Companies like Amazon will even give you a free one when you publish a book through them, though it puts your book in a different category. Note, however, that an ISBN is linked to whoever buys the number (like, say, the publisher...).

Even ebook companies like Smashwords will assign you one of their free ISBNs for your ebooks when you publish an ebook through them, so I use that. Free ISBNs are not the same as having your own, but I consider them good enough. Read up on the subject and see if it's something you want to shell out for.

As always, your choice.

Tag Lines and Blurbs

A tag line is simple, short, catchy, one-or-two-line phrase on the cover of a book or near the top of the back cover. On the front, tag lines are close to the titles, so they tell the readers the comment is about the book, not the author. They're also used in sales copy on sites for electronic sales. It is a great way to catch a reader's attention to check out a book.

Example: *When the party was just getting started, the screaming began…*

Example: *Fire had burned most of the world. One lone survivor undergoes a perilous journey for the secret to bring back civilization.*

Blurbs

Blurbs are those recommendations on books that praise the work of the author, either that book or previous ones. They're put there to pump up interest for prospective readers by saying that someone else (usually a respected writer) liked this. A blurb from some other famous writer, say Stephen King, can increase sales if people give it any credence. On traditionally published books, publishers will get other writers from their stable to blurb each other, even if the blurber has not read the book or author.

Blurbs can be one-liners for the cover ("*A mind-bending suspense thriller!*— Says best-selling author Harold Twombley"), or longer ones on the back cover. You'll see some books that even add bunches of them in the interior, which to me is overkill. I've never bought a book because of that. Good blurbs are nice to have, but good ones are tough to get, and completely optional.

For my books, I've been fortunate to have good writers I respect willing to say nice things about my work, and allow it to be used on my books. Here's one of the latest examples:

"*Reading Dale T. Phillips latest,* **A Darkened Room***, was a real treat. The author, who's best known for his bestselling hard-boiled Zack Taylor mysteries, is a master at old school hard-boiled tales. He's not breaking new ground in A Darkened Room, so much as paying homage to the old detectives that I know and love from years ago, like Robert B. Parker's Spenser. In fact, Zack Taylor might even be the new Spenser, and Dale Phillips, the new Robert Parker. It's a read that's at times tough as nails and other times sad and dark. But it's entirely filled with edge-of-your-seat suspense.*"

--Vincent Zandri, New York Times bestselling Thriller Award winning author of *The Remains*, *The Embalmer*, and *Primary Termination*.

A blurb like that is solid gold, from someone with real credentials. I read his blog, and followed the story of how he dealt with horrors of the traditional publishing world (one of the data points for why I went Indie). Another pro writer friend offered to introduce us via email, and Vin was gracious enough to grant a request for a manuscript read and offer this blurb. That's extremely generous help from a professional, and deeply appreciated.

Fellow writer friends are one thing, but if you'd like to reach out to get a blurb from someone more famous or well-known, *it's best if you have some connection.* Realize that most professional writers are busy, and don't usually relish being contacted out of the blue by a complete stranger who wants a favor, like their time and their name on a book from a writer no one has heard of. You're asking quite a bit for nothing, so why should they? Sometimes you can find them on social media and establish a connection first. Even so, it's forward to ask, but if that's your jam, feel free to go for it. But when they say no, accept that, and don't ask why.

Before you send someone a manuscript, make sure they've asked for it first. Never send a book unsolicited. Make sure that the book is professional, of high-quality (it better be really good), and in the genre the other writer works in. Don't ask a romance writer for a blurb on your high-fantasy epic (unless they also write that

161

under another name). Be polite, but not fawning or obsequious.

 Conferences and workshops sometimes offer opportunities to meet writers who might be approachable. If you can sit with one and establish a rapport (the bar or restaurant is best for this), there might be a chance for a polite request at some point, but use caution and good judgment. Don't be the jerk who goes around asking multiple writers to slap their name on a not-very-good first novel. Even I won't review a less-than-quality novel, and I surely won't blurb it if I don't think it's good. Before you commit a gaffe, ask your writer friends for advice.

And remember that many writers in traditional publishing usually will not blurb a writer who is not with their publisher. Competition, or they might not be allowed by their contract. So don't even ask them.

Keywords, Descriptions, Jacket Copy

This topic is critical to success and there are whole books on these particular subjects, with different schools of thought about the best ways to include everything. Browse the Resources Appendix for further information.

You're going to have to be very aware of where your book fits in the publishing world (category), because you'll need to add *keywords* (descriptive book tags) when you publish it. Each distributor allows you a certain number of keywords to include for your book, and of course you'll want the best ones. These keywords are critical for helping readers find your books, because that's what the big search engines use to locate the type of book you're selling. The more your book comes up in a search on certain keywords, the more chances you have of someone checking it out. So to sell more copies, learn what you need to keep your book search-term relevant. Search engines work on optimization, or SEO, which is why it's so important your book show up under a search on that keyword. One great tool that you'll want to look into for finding these in-depth is (KDP) Publisher Rocket.

Some say you should use all the characters allowed, and fill every category.

Descriptions and Jacket Copy are important as well, and they're used to quickly tell a browser if it's the type of book they'll be interested in. More detail than the tagline, they are included as part of the book listing online, and for a print book, on the back cover (jacket) at the top. Some distributors use two descriptions: a short one, about three sentences long, and a slightly longer one.

Here's the elements you should include:

- Hook the readers right away with a compelling first two lines.

- Make it easy and exciting to read- readers won't spend much time- they'll skim quickly to see if it's what they want.

- Establish what's at stake and make it important.

- Only a character or two, no more.

- Don't reveal everything- leave them wanting to know what happens.

To determine whether your descriptions are good, look for book descriptions of successful books that make *you* want to check out the book. What picture do they paint in just a few words that make it sound compelling? You'll want descriptions for your books that sound similar. Get help from your team, Beta readers, writing friends, etc. on what does well.

A disadvantage of *Smashwords* as a distributor is that the keywords and descriptions are the same for all distribution channels. Not a deal breaker, but important to realize. And in Amazon, the title, subtitle, and description are all searchable.

Dale T. Phillips

Distribution

These days, a writer no longer has to rely on just brick-and-mortar bookstores to sell their books. No more shipping, storage, returns, long delays for payment. The online world has been a boon, with everything available all the time. You can post a book, and have sales that very day, and get the money within weeks, not months. You might have more online sales than print in many cases, due to the convenience and lower prices of ebooks. Different demographics prefer different ways to access a story.

Of course the current online big dog is Amazon (and a lot of hate directed them because of it), through which you can sell print, ebooks, and audiobooks (via Audible.com- see the next chapter). Amazon is a powerful search engine, and where many go to find writers and books (and sure, other products) they like. Through Amazon, your books can be printed using Print-on-Demand (POD), the quick and easy way to get copies in just the quantities you need, without the old way of paying to have a printer set you up with 500-copy orders that sit in the garage.

The other major source for creating and distributing print books is Ingram, with their Lightning Source program. You'll want to study the pros and cons of publishing through both of these major distributors, and make your choices based on what you prefer to accomplish (you can also do both). Once your books have been published through these options, online sites of other major bookstores, like Barnes and Noble, and Powell's, will also list them.

There are some great ebook distributors, other than just the Kindle versions on Amazon. Kindle uses the *.mobi* file format, while Barnes and Noble uses the *.epub* format. Smashwords will take your file and convert it to different file formats, and sell it in those formats, so everyone can download it. It's a great site for giving away free books as well, by creating a coupon code which you can send to people for a free download.

Kindle has an exclusive program, called Kindle Unlimited (KU), where they want your ebooks sold only there. People differ on this, whether it's better to go all-in on the big dog or go wide, to have your books everywhere available. Feel free to research and experiment with different books, because you can sign any book up for a 90-day stint on KU, and see if anything changes significantly in your sales.

Another big player in ebook distribution is Draft2Digital, which gets your book into a number of other online book retail sites. It's another option that's quick and easy to use, and a terrific source for getting your book out to the world. Since this is a fast-changing world, other options may arise, so keep informed of what's happening in the publishing world.

Audiobooks

Since audiobooks are currently in the fastest growing book format right now, getting your novel out for sale as an audiobook is vital for success. If your book isn't, you're losing a lot, and leaving money on the table, as the expression goes. My audiobooks have sold hundreds and hundreds, and I love the continual income stream. Sadly, many writers from traditional publishers don't have their backlists up as audios, so they're missing out.

Reasons why you should have audio as part of your overall writing business strategy:

• Discoverability: Get a bigger audience and make it easier to find your work. Many potential fans like audio for a number of reasons, some just enjoying a good listen while walking, driving, running, or biking. You want all the fans you can get! These days, people have less time for reading print books, so audiobooks can be a saving grace. While *To Be Read* (TBR) piles are so big, chances are many readers won't get to your print book for a long, long time, **if ever**, but if you're on audio, they have a better chance of finding your work. If they like that one, they'll come back for more. Having your book listed in audio format also gets more hits in Internet searches, and is listed in more places, increasing your Internet presence, and the chances of someone finding your work. With over 10 million books in print and electronic format, your book is a drop in the ocean. There are far fewer audiobooks: smaller ocean, bigger chance to make a splash! And it'll get you into some extra markets. I was speaking with a person from a State Library about my books, and the first question was "Any of your books out on audio? Because we're investing in those right now."

• Sales: As well as finding new fans and watching your sales numbers increase, you can make money. Once the book is produced, all you have to do is promote it whenever you want. But each title is another product in your writer store, and even little trickles of money add up to an income stream. It's nice to have hundreds of sales in another venue.

• Reviews: While many print book reviewers are overwhelmed, there are many sites doing audio that can still accommodate a review. So you have more chances of getting good notice for your work. It all adds up. And listeners can also post reviews and ratings, which help.

• It'll make you a better writer: When someone else reads your words, it makes the clunky ones stand out, and the good ones sound better. Your ear will develop, especially for dialog.

• Freebies: With some audiobook production, you get free giveaway codes. You can gift these to reviewers, as contest prizes, or simply as rewards to readers. When someone buys a print book in person from me, I'll offer them the free audiobook as a nice extra.

Audiobook Options

Historically, audiobooks were done by professional companies and were expensive to produce, costing thousands of dollars. So only better-selling books made it. Now there are options.

• Someone ELSE does all the work- (and takes most of the money). While it's nice to have someone do all the work for you, as with traditional publishing, there's a danger. They might stick you with a hideous cover, a bad version, or a product priced wrong for the market, or take a long time to get it out- or never, while they hold the rights captive. In any case, it may not sell, and you're stuck. And when someone does the work, they also take most of the profit.

While you assume that a big publisher would do a professional version, there may be other factors. I got one from a BIG audiobook producer, but the narrator couldn't pronounce ANY place name in Maine correctly- even easy ones like Bangor and Augusta! So letting someone else do it all means the quality control may not be there, and there's little you can do about it. And you might tick off some fans. (I know I was!)

And that's assuming you can get a publisher to produce it. Professional narrators run upwards of $100 an hour, and it takes hours to produce a book. Plus other production costs, and packaging, and distributing, they're investing a few thousand dollars, at least. Since they expect a good return, they have to estimate the sales will exceed the output. So if you're a typical mid-lister, with less than ten thousand print/ebook sales per book, they may not even do your book for audio. But they'll likely still retain the rights, in case you hit it big. Then they can always do one later. But what happens is that you can go for years (or forever) without an audio version.

So- check your contract to see what provisions there are for audio. Even if you signed them away, and they're not doing anything with them, maybe you can re-negotiate. They may not give the rights back for free, but maybe you can offer them something for it that will make it worthwhile.

• Do it all yourself, keep all the money.

Two factors- Production and Distribution

It's true you don't need a studio anymore, so it's become cost-effective. You can produce high-quality audio files in different formats with free software and inexpensive equipment. I recommend Audacity software for recording, because it's free and simple to learn and use.

Are you a professional narrator? If you're charging money for the book, you want quality. Unless you're famous, the listeners may not be forgiving of less-than-awesome narrating. Before you start this path, do some voice work (maybe some podcasts), and get comfortable with a microphone and sound editing.

Drawbacks- while this can be done, the main cost is time to record and edit. Most of us don't have enough hours in a day now. And it may take hours of editing to get the sound to a professional level.

Distribution. Even if you do it yourself, how are you going to package, list, and sell the finished product? Tough to arrange this on your own.

- Work with a Service, and split the money

While there are other services, my current favorite production option right now is ACX.com, which feeds into Audible.com, an Amazon company. They make it easy and profitable for independents to get their books produced, listed, and sold. Better yet, the finished product is on the Audible site, AND on your Amazon book listing, right beside the print and kindle versions. Huge showcase! And they can tie it into *Whispersync*, which lets you switch between devices and formats.

Dale T. Phillips

How to Produce Audiobooks

For ACX, you'll need an account on the site (includes telling them where to send the money!).

1.   Check your publishing contract first, and beware of issues with anthologies, or other writers listed on your book as authors.

2.   **READ YOUR CONTRACT TERMS**! Audible gets an exclusive right for years, so make sure you're comfortable with the terms.

3.   Log in to ACX and search for your book, then claim it as yours, with the right to produce an audio.

Various ways to produce your book:

•   Do all the narration yourself. ACX distributes the book for you, and you make 40% of the list price.

•   Pay a narrator up front for doing your book. Narrators are expensive. While you can still retain your 40%, consider the cost, and how long it might take to recoup that. You post your project with the offer to pay, and get bids. Decide on who you want.

•   Offer a royalty split, for no up-front money- This is my favorite way. You are hoping that narrators will do all the work on spec, in hopes of making money when the audio sells. You each get 20% of the sale price in this part. They're putting in time, which to them equals hundreds, or even thousands of dollars, and you have no risk! But of course, you wrote the book, so your time is already invested.

When you've claimed your book, and decided if you want a narrator, you post it up as a project, with a description and notes on what the ideal narrator should sound like- male or female, age, accents, humorous, serious, scary, etc. You post an audition piece, a short segment that will give a good indication if the narrator is right for the work (dialogue with different voices is a good indicator). Add any helpful hints on what the passage should sound like.

This posts the project up for people to audition for, and you wait for replies. You can also search on available narrators, and sample their voices to see if any fit, then send them a message to see if they're interested in your project.

When auditions come in, listen if they're right for your work. When you've found someone who has the right voice for the job, you then set a schedule and make an official Offer. There's a date for a 15-minute milestone, which is a guide to see if they're on the right track, and a date for the project completion. You may need some back-and-forth on pronunciation and tone, and you send messages via ACX. When they're ready, they send ACX the files, and you give a listen. You can request changes if there's something amiss, so you have complete quality control.

When it's done properly, you Approve the work, which then goes through ACX *for their* approval, and then gets posted to Audible for sale. You'll need a cover image modified to their specs, a squared-off version of your book cover. Then it goes up on Amazon as well, linked with your print and Kindle versions. They will set the price of the finished book, based on length.

But there's more! ACX sends you codes for free downloads of the work. You can use these for reviewers, friends, giveaways, and rewards for your fans- it's an awesome way of promoting your work- for free! You send instructions and a download code, and someone gets the audio for free.

And the bonus program- if your work is the first someone selects when signing up for Audible, you get a bonus payment- it's split with your narrator, but is a nice addition.

Part Five

Setting Up the Marketing and Sales

Dale T. Phillips

Website

As an Indie writer, you're going to need a website, a good one. It's a necessary part of your business. It's how many people not familiar with you are going to find out about you, so it should be something that attracts them in some way. It's also going to boost you for search engines, which is a very desirable thing. Check out my full name on the big dogs of search engines, and my website comes up as the first hit-definitely something you want, especially when there are hundreds of other people with my first and last name whose sites come up when you don't add the middle initial.

Your website is an important part of your brand. When I hear of a new author, I first check out their website. If they've got outdated information from years before, they're missing out, and that's a mark against them. We need to see the latest and greatest, that they're actively involved with new production. You'll want to show off your cool book covers and convince someone to find out about you and hopefully buy something.

If you can't create a website by yourself, or have someone do it on the cheap or for trade, you'll have to spend some money. You don't have to go all fancy, but at least have a serviceable baseline. But— it has to look professional. Someone I know had a side business as a small publishing company, but an absolute joke of a website that screamed "Amateur." I pleaded with the owner, telling him that no serious person would deal with anyone hosting a site like this, but since it didn't cost him anything, he didn't want to invest. It cost him more in lost business, but he couldn't see it in those terms.

You don't need a lot: a simple splash (welcome) page, a page listing your works (with links on where to buy them), a page with a bio of you with any interesting facts (and yes, a picture- people trust faces), a contact page, an upcoming events/news page, and anything else you care to put in. You'll also need to put up an easy contact form which gleans the sender's email, to build your own fan email list (Mailchimp is a current popular method of keeping track). This is how you build success, along with related techniques.

Set it up so that you can make updates quickly and easily, without paying someone to do it over and over. You'll need a *hosting site*, a setup where your website resides. There are inexpensive options. Don't know website design? Then look up a dozen popular authors in your genre to see what they have. Don't copy, but create something similar.

Remember— for some fans and potential buyers of your work, this can be the first introduction they have to you. Make something fun, attractive, or compelling. Give them a reason to poke around the site. And make your books easily findable, in the proper order, with great links. If your books are in bookstores, list the bookstores with links to their websites.

Your upcoming books and appearances should be updated with regularity. When I see that a writer has an appearances page only with dates two years in the past, it makes me wonder what they've been doing since. You want to get people to your appearances, and let readers know of upcoming works.

On their website, or even their blog, some writers give away free stories, or other inducements to get readers coming back. This is an excellent way to acquire fans, if it doesn't take too much time from your writing for money.

Dale T. Phillips

Writers who offer helpful information, or want a contribution, will post a *Tip Jar* (via PayPal or other app), where visitors can click a link and donate a small amount as a contribution, via an online payment application. You can use *Patreon*, or a similar site, to get fans to sign up to contribute on a subscription basis. You can also sign yourself up as an Amazon affiliate, so that anyone going to Amazon from your site gets you a small credit if they buy something. Just don't put ads on your site (personal preference). It's tacky, and doesn't get you much. If it drives away a few fans, is it really worth it?

Blogs

You can also write a blog, if that's your thing, even though they're much less popular than they used to be. The blog can be linked to your website, with a similar theme, or completely separate. I still blog, and use it as a way of getting extra promotion for myself and many other writers. Several sites which distribute your books will also list your recent blog posts, so it's another chance for people to find out more about you. Some writers post thoughts here, or rants, lists of favorite things, fun articles, all kinds of material.

Marketing: Part One- Getting the Word Out

Marketing can be many things, but as used here, it's how you promote your book to the world. This chapter is how you use the Internet to get the word out to the world, primarily through electronic communication and public channels. The second part (next chapter) will be other ways in which you advertise you have something to sell. There are so many parts to marketing to success, and for every part there are multiple resources that go into greater detail: books, articles, blogs, videos, websites, and more. And different demographics prefer certain social media platforms, so if you're targeting, know where your audience goes to.

Part of your time as a successful author must involve marketing. The general rule (best practice) is 80% of your time writing to 20% spent on marketing- (though I'm happier spending about 90 percent doing the writing, and only 10 percent marketing). And most of what I do is one-offs and quick techniques, not the long, complex, involved campaigns, which are more lucrative, but require a greater amount of time and effort.

Writing is one job, and can be full time. While marketing can be done from your home or any computer, it can be a never-ending quest, taking up most or all of your time. Because it is true that the more good marketing you do properly, the more you'll likely sell, it's up to you to determine how much effort you're willing to put in. I've done a number of the options listed here. Sure, I could do more, and thereby sell more, but I didn't take up writing to be a *marketer*. My view is that I can do better in the long run by writing and publishing more good books than spending my time on yet one more technique that will sell a few more copies in the short term.

Never think that you must do a huge marketing push on every single book. Forget that. Do what you can. You're already too busy. You'll have to decide if it's worth the time and effort for you. As always, consider the Big Question: Would I be better off writing? Abbreviated as WIBBOW in the writing world.

Search Engines

If someone sees your name a time or two in connection with your book, it's not likely to stick. If they see it over and over again, they are more likely to check it out. The purpose of marketing is to get your book and your name out to the world. Discoverability is how potential readers discover your work. You want as wide a presence as possible on the World Wide Web, so it appears in results for your name or book title on Google, Bing, and other search engines. Links matter, and the more links to good results, the more discoverable you'll be. Tag other writers, and link to them, and you'll get some back. For example, I run author interviews on my blog, and help promote writers, which they then use for their own promotion, sending more traffic to my blog, which helps all around.

Some of the best results you'll want at the top when someone uses a search engine for your name:

• Your website— where they'll find links on where to buy for each book of yours

• Book distributors and sellers— Amazon, Barnes and Noble, Smashwords, Draft2Digital, others

• Blogs— your own, and others that mention you

• News— recent interviews, news stories about you, press releases, good promotion pieces

• YouTube videos— use this for interviews, book trailers, event videos. You can create your own channel on YouTube for these.

Dale T. Phillips

Social Media Sites

Social media sites are useful and sometimes effective,
but they require frequent content and interaction for
best results, and so can be a major time suck. So don't
try to leverage them all. Just do the top ones, the most
effective, or the ones you enjoy for other reasons.
You'll want some of the Resources to drill down on
each specific piece, to see how each site can be used
most effectively for the time you spend.

These sites work to connect you with others of similar
interest, and are a terrific networking tool. They all
come with risk, though, so always be aware of how you
involve yourself. You'll be posting personal information
out to the world. Apart from being a frequent target for
hackers, these sites gather a great level of detail about
you, so if you're concerned about privacy laws,
understand their terms of service, and what they can do
with your information.

Here's just a few of the big ones:

• Facebook— You'll want an Author page, separate
from your personal friend site. You can, if you wish,
create a separate page for your book titles, but if you
don't post much content there, what's the point?
Facebook has many author group and discussion pages,
with plenty of promotion opportunities, so it's good to

186

be found there. Also has many special interest groups and ad opportunities. Facebook videos are currently very popular.

• Twitter— This site is handy for tweeting short, free promotional event announcements, book publications, notices of special reviews, special deals, and tagging other writers. Some writers view their success by how many thousands of followers they have on this site.

• Goodreads— I'm calling this a social media site, because it's where many readers go to be social, listing the books they read and like, reviewing, rating, and commenting on same. You can post upcoming events, do giveaways, find Beta readers and other reviewers, run contests, join groups (genre and special interests), and post discussion points for readers to find. They supply widgets which allow readers to link to your book with one click.

Caution: before doing one of their Giveaways, read the fine print and study up.

• Pinterest— This site allows you to post images, and some writers pin their book covers along with other images, and get good results. Research to see if it's something that interests you enough to make it a part of your marketing routine.

• LinkedIn— Although this is a site for workplace professionals to network, some writers post their works and life updates here. Use with discretion if you're still in a workplace environment.

Online Bookseller Sites

Some distributor and bookseller sites allow you to post additional information, like your author photo and bio, upcoming events, blog posts, discussion points, and more. Take advantage of this. Amazon, for example, has an Author page for you to set up, where you can add extra material to your book listing. You'll want to fill these out, to make your book more appealing:

• Reviews— Post one or two of your best for the book, from reliable sources

• Product Description— The more compelling you can make this, the more likely someone will check it out

• From the Author— Add an author forward or some extra interesting information about the book: for example, if you've done some research

• From the Inside Flap— Here you can add a longer description, or some further enticing information

• From the Back Cover— Add a good blurb here

• Book series— Titles shown together, so if a reader likes one, they can see the rest.

Smashwords, the ebook site, allows you to post a bio, an author photo, and an interview- and you can create your own interview, answering the questions you give yourself. They'll let you post all your social media links, website, and blog links. They'll also let you post the print links to your books, which is rather generous, since all they sell are ebooks. And, like Amazon, they'll display your other works when someone accesses any one of them.

Bookstores with an online site will sometimes post your picture and website link, sometimes more, especially if you have a relationship with them, or are a local author. Check the ones where you know they sell your books, and ask to be listed if you aren't already.

Online Book Launches

With the spread of disease, and the curtailing of in-person book launches, the new normal is the online book launch. There is a great deal involved, so you'll have to learn how to do this properly. A starting point is the blog of Jane Friedman: https://www.janefriedman.com/how-to-throw-a-virtual-book-launch-using-facebook-live/

Public Print Media

There still exist a number of places to promote your work for the general public. While newspapers have crashed considerably in the last few years, some still exist. Concentrate on smaller local or regional publications around you that might publish your piece on local authors, genre authors to watch, specialty lists, etc. And of course, your book would be included in the piece you write. Some local newspapers still run articles and interviews with local authors. There are also regional newsletters of local events, so check if these exist in your area.

Local Television Stations

Many communities have televised community "bulletin boards," which detail upcoming local events. Include these for notification of your local book events. Along with that is local cable access television, which runs shows of local interest, and is usually looking for content. Some shows discuss books, and if there isn't one in your area, think about creating your own: having a friend interview you on camera, which you can send to the local station for possible airing— and many stations share content with other stations, giving you a much broader reach. So make a recording, and pass it to other stations. Add every appearance to your credits list and press kit, to show your commitment to local promotion.

Local Radio Stations

Another oft-neglected option is local radio stations, including independent and college stations. You might be able to score interviews on both and get great area promotion. I went on as a single-show guest for one station, and wound up doing 13 weeks of guesting to talk about writing and publishing.

Blog Tours

Some writer sites allow you to post a guest appearance on their blog as part of a virtual tour of different blogs. Some can be set up as part of a connected group. It might involve some time and effort, but you can get quite a broader reach by doing so, and be exposed to a whole new audience. Try to reuse as much content as you can, to keep from re-creating a new piece for every instance and thus taking up a great deal of your available time.

Podcasts

Currently there's a lot of interest in podcasting, so take advantage of that. Look for sites eager to host writer interviews and chats. You might even be tempted to start one of your own, hosting other writers and building a new audience.

Press Releases

A press release is a notice to the world that you have something to offer, as with a new book. These have easy guidelines for creating them, and sites that accept them. May not be worth a great deal of time, but they are useful, and one more chance to be discovered.

Ratings

Most of the major distribution/selling sites, as well as Goodreads, have ratings. Some people pay attention to ratings in any type of product. It's nice to have good ratings and reviews, and there are many ways to get them. Some writers spend a lot of time getting a pile of good ratings or reviews, which do help on places like Amazon. Also realize that there are many terrible ratings and reviews on sites from people who are simply jerks. Ignore the bad ones and get better ones from people that like your work.

Ads

Some sites, such as Amazon, Facebook, Google, etc., have advertising opportunities that you can pay for. Study up on these before you decide to put any money into this, and budget wisely. Chart your results to see what works and what's not worth it. BookBub is currently considered the gold standard by many, though is expensive and much more difficult now to get into.

Ad stacking is a coordinated effort to have ads in several places displayed at the same time, especially for book launches. The hope is that the multiple ads will boost the book ratings over a short period, enough for a noticeable jump. Another technique to research thoroughly.

Ads in other places, like in print? Don't spend a lot of money, because it's not effective, though I've run a few in conference programs, when it's cheap enough to get hundreds of targeted people to see the cover of your new book. As always, view the cost and time of what you're doing for the expected result.

Videos

Video book trailers are becoming more popular, but there isn't much evidence to show that they increase sales significantly. They're fun, and cool, and if you like doing them, and they're within your budget, it might be worth giving it a try and seeing what response you get.

Public Funding

Some writers with a good fan base have tried Crowdfunding, where they post a desired project and ask for donations to fund it, giving a stepped series of rewards for each donation level. There are a number of sites which support this, such as Kickstarter, GoFundMe, and others. Usually not effective unless you have that already established large fan base.

More Online Marketing Techniques

Some of the Resources books detail how to work your online presence in coordination with these techniques. These take time and careful study, but by experimenting and combining a variety of these, you can sell a lot of books.

• Pre-orders— This is making a campaign to set the book release to a certain date, allowing people to order it for that date. The hope is to cause enough of a sales velocity spike to get noticed (particularly by Amazon) for greater visibility.

• Campaigns— By preparing for a book launch months ahead, you can set up a number of timed events that will co-ordinate to bump your sales. Many options are available.

• Free/deep discount— Many sources say that if you have a series, offer the first one free or for a very low price, as a chance for more readers to discover you and want more of your books. If you only have one book, don't give it away for nothing, but only when you have others that they'll want to buy.

• Funneling— This technique is used to get readers hooked on your work by a process of converting them from getting material free to paying for it.

• Anthologies, bundling and box sets— These are great to put a bunch of your works into a well-priced set, or better, to team up with other authors, all cross-promoting. Best when themed, like all in a similar genre. Great way to get discovered by a whole new fan base.

• Giveaways— Contests and options to win a book can generate some excitement and interest, so experiment with this option to see if you can convert to increased sales.

Comparative Titles

One thing to check out is titles and books that are like yours. Use this in your marketing: "if you liked x best -

seller, you'll enjoy <mine>." Or think of the Hollywood idea of high-concept: mine is x meets with y, with both x and y being big-sellers.

Good blog to check out: Nathan Bransford-https://nathanbransford.com/blog/2018/04/how-to-come-up-with-good-comp-titles-for-your-book

Marketing Part Two: Other Material

Some writers spend a lot of time and money on promotional swag: bookmarks, postcards, pens, coffee mugs, hats, T-shirts, golf tees, cupcakes, printed frisbees, tension squeeze balls, whatever. Sure, I sometimes take one of them at conferences, but usually wind up throwing most away without further action. Some great advice from Indie Publishing guru Joe Konrath was to not waste your time or money on any marketing or ad that doesn't work on you, to make you want to check out a book. We saw one table at a conference with loads of this stuff on display for the taking. He pointed to it and asked, *"Does any of that make you want to check out or buy that book?"* We said *no*, proving his point. If it's not selling you books, don't spend money on it.

Newsletters

Newsletters are a necessity to many big sales gurus, for connecting with fans and keeping in contact to let them know what's upcoming. If increasing sales is your goal, study this further and learn the techniques of getting email signups and grooming those fans. For signups, offer something free to those who agree to receive your newsletter, and never misuse that list for other ads or spam. *Mailchimp* is currently a good way to manage email lists, free for the first 2000 names. There are others, and more arising all the time. Author David Gaughran (see the Resources Appendix) will tell you most of what you need to know in this area.

Branding

Branding is how you present yourself to the world, what people think of when they hear your name. It involves every book, every interaction, everything you as an author do. Lots to absorb, so do some deep learning on this, if you want to sell more books.

Dana Kaye has books on the subject, and there's a terrific post by author and marketing guru Joanna Penn. Much more help if you enter "Branding for Authors" as an Internet search term.

Part of your brand is your **author tagline**. Describe what you do as a writer in one short sentence, and make it memorable. You want people to recall your name and genre, and interested folks to check further. Mine is "*Scary books and murderous crooks.*" Short, punchy, and it indicates both my mysteries and horror genre pieces. Try your tagline out on other writers and fans, to see what sticks.

Press Kit

One item to put you ahead of most others, establishing yourself as a professional, is a *press kit*. Look up how to create a useful and quality one. Having it to send to prospective sites is a huge advantage. It's great for interviews and appearances, presenting all the available information so that people can easily promote you without having to do any actual work. They'll often just take the information you display in this and repost it.

Essentially, it's an item to promote you as a package, and should include the following:

- Author picture

- Short bio

- A few upcoming and past events

- Books available

- Credits

- A short blurb or tagline for media to repeat

Business Cards

You *must* have writer business cards, with your website and some sort of tagline on them, even maybe an eye-catching book cover. These are critical for handing out at every opportunity. I still encounter writers who don't have them, and they've missed an opportunity for sales and promotion. Every time you meet someone who seems at all interested in your work, they get a card. Get a haircut? Ask the barber or hairdresser if they read. A yes response gets a card, and a quick spiel. I sold two complete series doing this, and got two new fans! Eating at a restaurant? Ask the server if they like to read, and you know the rest. See someone reading a book? If they look up, you might be able to start a conversation about what they like to read. A card is a non-obtrusive method of slipping someone an easy reminder to check you out later. If you meet another writer, always ask for theirs as well, as reciprocity is appreciated. For me, since I do writeups of author events, it's a great way for me to remember who I met and how to find them and link to them. Those without cards have often been left out.

And swap cards with other writers at every opportunity. Connect, connect, connect. Cross-promote and help others.

Publicist

You can hire a publicist to help get the word out about your books, but make sure you're getting value for your money. Some writers even offer a percentage of sales rather than a flat fee, which seems better. Ask them what they will do, what paths they will pursue, and what the expectations are. Remember the rule about how contracts protect everyone, by laying out expectations, pay, and details about what will happen.

Shelf Talker

In bookstores, they have something called a "shelf talker," a card that describes one of the books on the shelf. It's usually an exciting description and maybe some glowing review. They're usually created and placed by the bookstore staff, for books they enjoy and think are good, a little something to make a book of quality stand out. You can create your own, though, and for a bookstore you've established a relationship with, ask them to place it by your book.

Banners/Signs

For several years, I got extra attention by putting up a poster at author events, with my picture, and several titles on it. Most other authors had nothing of the kind, so I stood out in a good way. I've since upgraded to a professional-looking, six-foot banner, a splashy display that really catches the eye. One more thing to grab the notice of a passerby and induce them to check out your offerings.

Flyers

As stated, fliers are a great inexpensive method to spread the word for a local upcoming event, and I use a standard page size to make mine. Libraries will usually post these if asked, as will many bookstores and some other businesses. Include clear details on who, what, when, and where. Post both physically and the image on the Internet.

Get Creative

Chuck Palahniuk once gave out imitation severed limbs at a book signing, keeping in theme with one of his works. Some signings are done in costume. Some have themed food to offer. You can have contests, do funky ideas that involve fun, and get people wanting to attend your public events.

What else can you do to grab the interest? My wife found a company that would put an image on a tapestry for a low price, so I have several book cover images on tapestries that make a nice table cover or hanging banner. One more thing to set you apart from the rest. For one terrific promotional tool, I also give out a trifold pamphlet, which shows my book covers, has a short description of each book, and sales and contact information, in one neat takeaway. They go like hotcakes at author events, where people can check it out later for buying, because not every browser wants to commit on the spot.

This may contradict the advice on not spending money on swag that doesn't work, but if it's cheap and fun and different and catches the eye enough to make someone give a look, try it and see what happens. In Indie, we get to experiment all the time to see what works.

Dale T. Phillips

Speaking in Public

Many authors are introverts. And reluctant to make public appearances, as fear of speaking in public is one of the most common fears. Some just don't prefer to be out and about. Which makes selling their books in person that much harder. For those who want to feel more comfortable with public speaking, find your local chapter of *Toastmasters International* to learn how to do it better, or a local community education course in public speaking. Practice makes you improve quickly. Each appearance gives you more confidence, and the feedback you get can shape you into a person comfortable to be in front of a crowd.

Some authors think that their limited time is better spent writing, or other activities, rather than pressing the flesh and connecting with live readers. To each his own. In our new world of publishing, you can sit in a room and only connect via the Internet, and never have to see another fan in person again, if that's your choice. But to reach a broader audience, it's great to make connections, to let people see a live author.

You might get the chance to be on radio, local television, or a podcast, and these are excellent ways to reach an audience. It's good to get comfortable talking about your work, and to think of a few things that would interest the listeners. Many times you can chat with the host before the show, to get some idea of potential topics. Always come prepared, when you can. Good practice keeps you from being nervous, and helps you to sound confident.

There are so many places for an author to meet the public. Here's a few tips:

• Have a copy of your book on display, so they can see the cover. It's a good one, right? If you're on camera, hold it up so people can see the title and cover.

• Many author appearances are centered around reading from their work, but please, if you insist on this, keep it short! Far too many authors drone on to a room as the audience gets sleepier, like in a boring lecture. Pick an exciting section of the book, something with action, or conflict, and end with some sort of cliffhanger that makes the audience desperately want to buy the book to find out what happened.

• You do better when you engage the audience. Try to imagine what would entertain them, and prompt them to ask questions (have a couple of your own as backup). Tell them stories or find out what stories they like, what prompts them to pick up a book, and what they pass on to other people. Talk *to* them, not *at* them.

- Any liquid you have at hand should be in a small-mouth container. Don't make the mistake of gulping from a big bottle, and having liquid sploosh all over you. While funny, some would prefer not to embarrass themselves like this.

- Give them a little something back. These people took time out to come and see you. Offer a free ebook, a discount, a special story they can access, something. Take pictures of your audience and post them, so they can see themselves, and tell their friends. You want people talking about your appearance, and sharing on social media!

- Act like a pro. Dress well, comport yourself well, and be courteous to everyone. Even if they ask stupid questions. Even if some rude doofus walks through while you're talking, as happens at many author readings. Your display should reflect your status as a pro. If it looks cheesy and amateurish, your books will seem not as good. If your display is classy and professional, you'll impress people and get more sales.

- No matter how small the crowd, give your best talk and make it matter. Don't despair at having only a person or two in attendance- it happens. Now's your chance to knock their socks off and get a fan for life.

There are so many venues to meet and greet the public, so let's run through a few.

- The Book Launch— This is the best, where people come to see just you (and maybe another author or two) and your new book. Whatever the venue, it's all about you, so it's flattering to have a crowd. Here's where you shine the best, maybe do a short reading, entice the crowd with the shiny new work. Have an anecdote or two about what makes this book special, and another about your journey as a writer. Be entertaining, give them something for coming out to see you. And make sure you've advertised this heavily, so that you shoot for a better turnout. If your author friends have local book launches, go and support them. They might do the same for you someday.

- The Convention/Conference— At many conventions and conferences, there are opportunities to speak on a panel with other authors, to an audience, on a variety of subjects. This is a great way to get yourself introduced to a roomful of people, and to hone your chops talking about books and writing. And you usually get an opportunity to sign books afterward. I've made significant sales from this, from people who liked what I said on the panel coming up afterward to the signings.

- The Bookstore Appearance— Many independent bookstores know that having live Indie authors come in and give talks is a great way to get more book buyers into the store. So work yourself up a good press kit and start contacting the local ones. Many are delighted to have you come in for an afternoon or evening talk. It's a win-win.

- The Library Appearance— As with bookstores, many libraries are happy to have you come in and give a talk. Many will let you sell books afterward. As writers, we should help libraries every chance we get, so contact them with suggestions for good talks. You know how to get on their good side? Donate a book or two for their collection. You get a write-off, and your work gets to a broader audience, many times with recommendations by the staff. If you get good enough, you can even get paid for an appearance, as some libraries have a fund for special projects. The Speaker's Bureau of Sisters in Crime is one ongoing program that gets us into many libraries, and pays us to do so!

- The Schools— Know how many schools have writing classes, all the way through college, with young people eager and hungry to learn about writing? More than you can get to. Give it a shot, see if it's your thing. Especially good if you have a book targeted for the age range you're speaking to.

- The Book Club— This can be a smaller, more intimate group, a dozen or less. But of these groups who invite you usually have most, if not all, of the people who have read your book and want to discuss it. Sales may be fewer, but these are power book-readers who tell others what they like. If they like you, you'll definitely make more future sales.

There are others, so this is just a sample of the many opportunities you have of meeting potential new fans. It's not about how many copies you sell at each one, it's about building your professional writer foundation. If even a fraction of the people you meet buy a good portion of your current and future work, you'll do well.

Dale T. Phillips

Signings and Face to Face

For public appearances, few things beat a good book signing. These can occur at bookstores (most common), or at any venue you can set up in person: festivals, craft fairs, anyplace where you're allowed to sell books for the day and the public can come by. They're a great way to meet people and sell books. I've done signings at conferences and all over New England, from cow fields to village greens to yacht clubs, and acquired many new fans that way.

With so many of these around, indoor and outdoor, you have myriad opportunities to put up a booth and sell, as hundreds of people walk by. At many, you'll have a product that's different from most or all the rest of the event. Since many people go to these looking for gift ideas, put up a sign that says "Books make great gifts!" Sometimes there's a cost to participate, but the rewards can be terrific. Some fairs, you won't do so well, others you'll think you struck gold. Find those that work for you.

Some writers complain that book signings are not worth it, to go to a place for several hours and only sell a few books. If that's your frame of reference, it may not be the best use of your time. If you're shy, it can even be a burden. To me, making that personal connection with people is a good chance to find a new lifelong fan. If you have more books out, especially a series, you'll likely get future sales from those you encounter, not just for that day. Some will check you out, to buy later. And some bookstores will even take consignment copies or buy a few to stock after the signing.

Once you've established a relationship with a bookstore, you can have the conversation about a signing. The smart ones love them, because it costs them nothing, and potentially brings in more customers. Some will ask how you'll promote, because they want some kind of assurance that people will show up. So in the run-up to your event, you're going to get the word out and try to convince others to show up while you're there. And if you get a crowd at a bookstore, and make some sales, the store will want you back for more. Holiday-themed books do well when timed properly. Weekends are usually the best time, for more foot traffic makes for more potential customers. But you might have to do some at other times less desirable.

Advance promotion helps a great deal, and many bookstores and libraries hosting a signing will make up advance flyers with your author photo, the time of the signing, and maybe a title or two or yours. You can spread these around in public places to notify people. Post it on your blog and website, if you have them. Cross post to social media with the image of the flyer. If they venue doesn't have one, make up your own.

Understand, though, you may get times when the crowds are few, but it's nothing to get discouraged about. Even famous authors sometimes get small numbers attending theirs— it happens. I've had snowstorms and downpours and monster heat waves that killed a few signings. If you get stuck with something like that, don't fret, and don't whine to the bookstore people (or event organizers). Accept it and schedule another one to make up for it. Always thank the staff, and anyone who has helped set up the event. Others like to be appreciated for their effort.

What should your signing table look like? It may be a simple card table and a chair, or a more elaborate setting. Check with the venue on what you can set up. My signing space is now big, filling a long table with books and marketing material, with a banner to the side. People remark on how impressive it is, and it catches the eye, as it's meant to. So I sell more books at these events than many others. The longer people stop by to check out your wares, the more likely they are to buy something. Have enough for them to look over for more than a quick glance.

Here's some of what you might bring:

• Books— On the table top, I put only a single copy of each book, rather than stacking them in piles. While some stores may purchase copies in advance, I offer to bring my own as consignment, and take away unsold ones at the end. This way no one has to deal with shipping costs, lost or misplaced or undelivered copies, and the store doesn't worry about getting stuck with unbought copies. Also, I always have enough, though I've seen many an event where the hapless author didn't have copies, because they relied on someone else to deliver their books. Ouch. Don't allow liquids or food to be put near your books, because if there's a spill, you might be out some money for ruined copies.

• Table— Will the venue provide one, or should you bring your own? I usually pack one the size I need, just in case. Anything might happen, so it's better to be prepared.

• Cover cloth— Always bring a covering cloth, because you never know what you'll get. Something that's attractive or a conversation piece is better. I use one of my unique book-cover tapestries to cover the table as added promotion. Another author uses the flag of the country featured in her books.

• Chair— Because I don't want to take the chance of getting stuck sitting for hours in a rickety or uncomfortable chair, I pack my own chair for comfort.

• Bookstands— These are cheap and easy to get, and make the book stand up to catch the eye, rather than lying flat. Wire, plastic, whatever you want, but prop those titles up for better visibility.

• Marketing material— Not everybody buys on the spot, some take your information away to check out later. Business cards, book marks, pens, coasters, whatever you've got. I have a trifold pamphlet with all my books listed, with covers and descriptions and where to buy, and pass these out at many events.

• Banner— Stand-up or attached banners that advertise your work really grab the eye, and cost less than you might think. They're a real attention-getter, and I feel worth it.

• Sign-up sheet— Offer something free for those willing to put down their email for your newsletter and email list for new book notifications. I offer a free ebook or audiobook as incentive if they sign up. You can also say 'Enter to win prizes,' and give something away. Always have one or two other names filled in first- don't put out a blank sheet, as no one wants to be the first on that.

- Writing implements— Bring some pens to write things down, sign your email sheet, and of course, sign books!

- Candy/food/lunch— If you'll be there through lunch, or for several hours, you may want to bring something to eat, as long as the venue allows it. Some authors give out cookies or treats (get the okay first), and if it's a place where kids might show up, a small bowl of candy treats is a nice touch.

- Water/liquids— Though some venues may provide this, don't assume, and bring a couple of bottles for yourself. You can get mighty thirsty talking to people for several hours.

- Camera/phone—Take pictures of your table setup, your fans, the venue, fellow authors (if any) and post to social media, and let the venue know about it. Especially for bookstores, who love the promo. Offer to send a fan the image of them getting a book signed, and they can further promote you!

- Square/Change— If you're signing at a bookstore, they'll likely handle the purchases, but for fairs and craft festivals, you'll want small bills for change, and some sort of credit card or money transaction software, maybe *Square* or *PayPal* or *Venmo*. And decide in advance if you want to take checks.

- Conversation pieces— Some authors bring extra fun stuff: things mentioned in their books, or associated in some way with the genre. Western writers could put out cowboy hats, sheriff badges, or a lariat or saddle. Horror writers may put out something scary, like a fake human skull. Children's authors go for stuffed animals or toys. Anything to provide a conversation starter as an opportunity to chat and make a connection.

• Outdoor shows— I bring a 10x10 canopy to provide shade and shelter.

• Other items— Duct tape is always handy to have around for fixing things with a quick repair. Have a supply of tissues or napkins on hand.

• Consignment forms— I always bring my own, in case the venue doesn't have theirs handy.

Things to Note

People will buy more from people who are likable. Be approachable and interested when people walk by. Some authors sit behind their table with sour expressions or bury their face in their phone, book, or laptop, and don't look up unless someone is practically standing on them. Greet people and engage in polite conversation. If they glance at the books, ask *"what do you like to read?"* Their answer gives you a place to point them to something they might like, even someone else's. If they say they don't have time to read, mention your audiobooks. But if they say they don't read, well, they probably won't buy. If they answer with something you don't have, try to give them a good suggestion (especially in the bookstore), or point them to a relevant author at big multi-author signings.

Don't hang all over them while they're looking, and let them alone if they're checking out the books. Don't go for the hard sell. At non-bookstore signings, if people are debating on two (or more) different books, offer a discount or a package deal. Works quite a bit of the time. If they're a little short of funds, let it slide, if it's the difference between a sale of a book and having them walk away without a book of yours. You want and need that new reader more than an extra buck or two.

Face to Face

Meeting the public is a mixed bag. You'll find some people who are very nice, some who are downright rude, some who have obvious issues, and some who just want to talk for a long time to anyone who will listen. Always be polite and gracious, and if you need to break away, excuse yourself to do so (the fake phone call is a great excuse to get out of an awkward conversation). Having done a lot of events, I can mostly tell who will buy and who will not just from a person's approach to the table.

Check your appearance in the mirror before signings and meeting people. Make sure to have tissues or something similar on hand, just in case. If you eat during the event, make sure you don't have bad breath or food showing between your teeth afterward. Look nice, like a professional.

Always be Ready

It's important to be prepared, and always have books available when you leave your home. While it's kind of an old cliche about selling books from the trunk of your car, remember than best-seller John Grisham did just that when he started out. I've sold many at "impromptu signings," where people have asked for a copy on the spot. At one place, a fan rushed to buy the latest as soon as I pulled up, and three more people who saw this got interested, and bought copies. So keep a few copies in your vehicle.

At writer conferences, have a copy of at least one (with a great cover) to show around when people are about and chatting. It helps a lot to share, so be sure to ask about their work as well.

A writer friend accompanied me to an event where I was on a panel. When other panelists didn't show, I got her a spot, and she rose to the occasion, and had a chance to sell some books!

Trading

It's important to make ties with other writers, so when I meet someone new, and we talk about our books, I'll usually offer a trade, by swapping my book for one of theirs. It's a great, inexpensive way to check out someone else's work, and if it's good, I'll usually offer them an interview on my blog, along with a review. It's a win-win for everybody, but the traditionally-published authors miss out, as they cannot trade, because their publisher wants full price for every book, no swaps allowed.

Dale T. Phillips

Targeting Fans

Go to the sites where your fans go, and market to there, if you can. Many successful writers say it is important to do at least a modicum of market analysis, to identify your ideal reader fan, the type of person who is most likely to buy your work. Branding is critical, because it defines the fan type for the genre. For example, if you're a science fiction author, you'd want to sell to your target audience at science fiction conventions and like-minded gatherings. It can certainly help you market your book, and remember, each new fan may buy multiple books. People who like your work will also tell others, and may give you good reviews. Finding new fans is important, so put some time into this study. And when you get a new fan, the continued connection is important. Newsletters let you do this in a positive way, letting fans know more about you and what you have to offer. Email distribution lists are important, so do some research into the depth of details involved in that.

Affinity Marketing/Tie-ins

If you feature a particular hobby or industry or activity in your books, you should think about *affinity marketing* and *tie-ins*, appealing to those who enjoy that aspect. For example, many popular cozy mysteries feature recipes, which add to how the author can talk about the book and interact with fans who have tried and commented on the recipes provided.

Authors need every advantage marketing against other books, and marketing to other loves reduces the steep odds. Tie-ins may also have media outlets. From knitting to horses, those hobbies or industries are always looking for content for articles. Being featured as an author who loves to knit (or a mainstream author who really knows her horses) is catnip to editors looking for a fresh take on that subject.

One successful Indie author has horses as a big part of her books, so she attends equestrian shows, and sells a great many copies, because she's selling something the people know a lot about, and they can talk for a long time about just that. Another author details a particular country, so she attends ethnic festivals for those folks, and sells like hotcakes. Books featuring martial arts might sell at places where they teach that activity. A debut author has a baseball-themed mystery, and does a lot of promotion based around that. They're all great at targeting particular audiences.

A book may *not* appeal to fans of an activity, though. For example, a popular mystery writer wrote a mystery featuring golf that didn't sell well. The comment was "golfers don't read mysteries, and mystery readers don't golf." (Though I do both.)

Helpers

Some recommend developing "street teams," groups of superfans who help you promote during book launches and such. The idea is that they're involved with the author so deeply that they'll do things to help push a book or author, especially during coordinated events. I'd love to have other people work for me, but don't put in the time or effort to push this. Good idea, though if you can make it happen.

Organizations and Groups

There are a great many writer organizations and groups that can help you reach success. Genre groups, like the *Mystery Writers of America*, the *Sisters in Crime*, the *Science Fiction Writers of America*, the *Romance Writers of America*, and many others. There are state and regional groups for writers, and these can play a part in helping you with valuable resources, contacts, and potential readers. I've found boosts for my career by participating in a number of different organizations. Many have conferences, classes, workshops, and seminars to help you improve your craft.

Some are involved in awards, so being a part of them helps you understand how awards are done. Some have agent meetings and pitch sessions, so if that's your goal, you can get closer to it. There are opportunities to speak on panels, present topics for discussion, and learn from each other. And many organizations post member book listings on their websites and in their newsletters, so you get a lot of exposure with your release, to a targeted audience.

The social aspect is important as well. Events like talks and lunches and parties. It's nice to have people around you who can speak your writer language, to share experiences, resources, and tips. You can make good friends and not feel so isolated as a writer. I get charged up at writer conferences, inspired and waiting to get back to working on another bit of writing.

Getting involved is the best way to further yourself. Be an active participant, and this will help to get your name out there. Take on a role within the organization, and help others. You'll find it's rewarding when other writers appreciate what you do.

Connect with other writers, who can become your champions. Connect with them and review their work, promote them on multiple social media platforms. Comment on their blog posts, congratulate their wins.

One other group you should develop is book clubs. These gatherings are useful for getting numbers of fans. I've been a part of some, and spoken to others. They tend to be voracious readers, and helpful for giving feedback and providing part of a fan base. Our local library offered us a chance to put together a package for regional book clubs, with a few donated copies, some marketing material, and a set of discussion points. Great possibilities to expand your profile.

Schools are an excellent way of finding more potential readers. This works best if you have something aimed at the proper age range, such as YA or children's novels, but you can also speak to writing classes and talk to them about writing and publishing. Teachers have asked for material to present to their classes about writing, students have requested other pieces, and I've given out a few of those.

Teaching and Talks

Apart from *talks* at schools, you might even get to *teach* courses at schools, night schools, local colleges, community education classes, or even online. Teaching at a prison may also be an option, and I know one successful Indie writer who does that.

Other groups, such as Senior Centers, sometimes welcome authors to come in and give a talk. Authors with age-related books, such as caregiving, or topics of interest such as travel, will be able to find opportunities. Any outside clubs a writer may belong to, such as Toastmasters, Mensa, the Elks, or whatever, may also offer a chance to give a talk.

I've taught workshops and led groups on different aspects of writing. One big opportunity came when I received an offer to teach at a Summertime Writer's Conference! Attendees had seen me speak on panels at another conference, and recommended me. I had a lovely and lucrative time teaching two different several-day classes on various writing aspects. There are many writer conferences that provide opportunities. To pursue this, develop your area of expertise and submit proposals.

Bookstores

Most of us writers love poking around bookstores, hoping to find undiscovered treasures and pleasant surprises. We grew up waiting for the day our books would be seen on the shelves of bookstores, or better yet, the front windows. In the past, that was the primary way to reach readers, other than a rack in a few retail chains, drugstores, airports, etc. (if you could get onto those racks in the first place). You could also order print books through the mail.

Then one day, not so long ago, disruptive technology changed the game. You could buy electronic books online (ebooks): inexpensively, conveniently, delivered immediately. You had immediate access to a story. And you had more stories to choose from than could ever fit into a physical store. Best of all, you could buy more books with your limited budget. In one fell swoop, the world was different. Many people who didn't live near good bookstores or libraries could now get just about anything they wanted. They were happy, and books were sold to more people.

First, this new path was ignored by the traditional book industry. Years ago, there were many fine companies who cared about books, but later some people got the bright idea that books were just widgets, and a company that could become big could make tons of money. So they started conglomerating for the sake of pure profit, until there were just six big ones left (now The Big Five or Four, and mostly owned by overseas multinationals). This was not a good thing for quality books. *Popular* became far more important than *good*, giving us tomes by less-than-stellar writers.

The Manhattan industry relies on pushing non-returnable paper books, mainly to bookstore chains. Then the *chains* wanted to go mega-sized, and they started conglomerating, gobbling up all the smaller places, and driving many independent bookstores out of business. Barnes and Noble crushed numerous locally-owned bookstores- which is rather ironic, since they now pose themselves as the virtuous victims of Big Bad Amazon, who they say is trying to destroy Book Culture.

The odd thing is, locally-owned, independent bookstores are now making a comeback (at least they *were* before the Great Plague- many will not survive now)- despite the increased competition for dollars, the public craves good stories, and often will support their local store instead of going online to save a few bucks. This is great news for modern-day writers, for a smaller, locally-owned bookstore is more likely to stock a local author than the big mega-chain, who relies on New York publishing best-sellers.

Bookstores need Indie writers more than the Indie writers need bookstores.

Say what? Yeah, with the advent of ebooks, and a number of online places to buy, every author now has access to a worldwide market that's open 24/7/365. And not just Amazon, there are many more places. If all a physical brick-and-mortar store stocks are books popular to New York, why shop there? *Buy local* is a modern slogan, to keep your purchasing dollars close to your home community. And it's a great idea when both the writer and the store are local. Win-win. Buyers are directed to their store, and support the local fan base. A writer will send fans to a store rather than to a computer.

Sounds great, right? Let's take a closer look. First, there's not a lot of profit in print books. Making a living writing them or selling them is a tough row to hoe. Ideally, you want both the producer of the book and the vendor of the book to make something. But with razor-thin margins, that can be a tough thing to pull off. For a store to make enough money to be worth it, bookstores ask for a (usually) 40% discount off the cover price, that being their share of the pie. Your books had better be priced so there's something left over for you, or you could wind up losing money on each sale (my case when I was published by a small press).

Know the answer to this before you walk into a bookstore, because you'll be asked— *where are your books listed*? Most chain bookstores buy from big wholesalers like Ingram. Though independent booksellers also buy from wholesalers, they'll sometimes buy books from Indies or more likely take them on consignment. Some will froth at the mouth if you mention *Amazon*. Since most of the Indie world is Print-on-Demand (POD), we'll focus on this type.

•   If you are POD with IngramSpark, you are listed in the Ingram Wholesaler database.

•   If you select "Extended Distribution" at Amazon, you are also listed in the Ingram database, because extended distribution means that Amazon has your book in their IngramSpark account.

Since most local authors aren't well known, the store doesn't know if the books will sell. So rather than buy outright, a risky proposition, many will take consignment books, agreeing to give the books shelf space and only paying the author after the books sell. This means the author assumes the monetary risk and fronts the cost of the printed books in hopes of a return many months down the road. Not a problem, but suppose you have a few titles, and want to appear in a number of area bookstores? Say they take 3 of each title in each store, which means your floated cost is now in the hundreds of dollars. So you have to adjust your business to account for that. Without some sort of buzz, your book is one among hundreds, or thousands on those shelves. How are people going to find your book? By randomly wandering and happenstance? You've got to do more things to get noticed.

Some bookstores want to charge Indies- one well-known venerable and ancient bookstore in our area charges Indies $100 *just to place the books on the shelf.* I'd tell them where they could stick their bookshelf- I know the place ain't gonna sell so many of my books to make that worthwhile- they're counting on their cachet and snob value, and taking advantage of desperate Indie authors. Other places charge much smaller fees for special call-outs, like premium Local Writer placement, but unless they are moving a good number of books for you, it may not be worth it.

If your books don't sell, the store will justifiably want you to take them back. Shipping is expensive, or you can physically get them. So it's all time and effort. Transporting physical books to physical locations can be a chore. And you don't just show up out of the blue and expect a place to bend over backwards to help you out- you have to develop a relationship. You're like any business, which has to maintain constant contact with your vendor. And with a few bookstores, you could spend a lot of time just doing that. You'll have to spend valuable time chatting them up, and seeing what else they offer, and occasionally buying. After all, if you go online to buy, why should the store support you?

As a businessperson, you have a limited amount of time for writing, promotion, marketing, and living. You'll have to calculate whether it's worth your time and effort to cultivate lasting partnerships with more than one or two places. And if you're difficult to work with, or don't bring in much business, they soon won't want to work with you. I've heard of Indie authors going into a bookstore and acting like jerks, demanding signings, shelf placement, etc. Nothing turns a bookstore off quicker.

So you've got to up your game. When I find a new local bookstore, I go in to chat, give them a copy of my marketing pamphlet (shows I'm a pro with good material, and the cover illustrations also show professionalism), tell them about local appearances, mention my organizations and connections, offer to send a press kit, all of which shows I'm a cut above.

And of course, I'll have some good-looking books to show as examples. We'll discuss the possibility of a store book signing, and I mention how much promotion I do on social media, how, after each event, I do a blog writeup, with links, which then goes out to several platforms to thousands of people. I'm letting them know they get a lot of promotion by working with me, and so make it easy for them to say yes. Work on getting a book signing at the store, which helps both you and them. Promote the place, boost the profile of the author and the store. Make the store THE place where readers can connect with writers (along with libraries). Show them that you as an Indie author help their profits. Give them good reasons to work with you and other Indies. After you're in a few bookstores, you can chart some of your sales, as they report to *Bookscan*, and your Amazon author account shows you the sales from that.

In closing, your book is a representation of you as an author, and should represent quality. A crappy cover and obvious errors aren't going to convince a store that you're ready to compete for shelf space with glossy professional products. Be a pro in all your dealings, and for goodness sake, keep track of all your product out among your vendors. You'd like to make a little profit, at least.

Dale T. Phillips

Libraries

Libraries are for readers, and one of the best places for you to get your books into. Once readers find your work, if it has merit, they'll come back for more. And they'll tell fellow readers about it.

So how do you get Indie-published print books into libraries? By knowing how they order, and getting your books into *that* system. Libraries buy from certain places: Baker & Taylor, Ingram, and a few others. Make sure you're listed in those distributors. There are dozens of books and articles on this, so check a few out, and see if that's a path you want to follow. It's work, but it can be done. Here's one link for you to get started: https://www.thecreativepenn.com/2019/06/12/book-marketing-how-to-get-your-book-into-libraries/

WorldCat is the world's largest network catalog of library content and services. WorldCat libraries are dedicated to providing access to their resources on the Web, where most people start their search for information. If a library vetted your book, it will be here. Other libraries can order it, knowing it's already been approved by a library-less work for them. This is a reason to donate your books to a local library, to get it listed.

So once your book is listed, how do you get a library to order it?

• Go in person (best), phone, or via email, and request to speak with the person in charge of ordering new books. Explain who you are, show your professional credentials, and see how receptive they are. If they can find your book in their wholesaler system, you stand a much better chance.

• Get patrons of that library to request your book.

• Take part in local author events sponsored by the library. Our local one has a big author presentation every year, showcasing local writers. If yours doesn't yet do that, offer to help set one up!

• Outside author programs- one of the organizations I'm a member of a Speaker's Bureau, where we're (usually) paid to appear on a library panel as part of their special programming, lecturing or putting together a mystery from audience suggestions. It's a lovely way to connect.

• Book clubs- many libraries have connections with a local book club, so check that out. We were given the opportunity to donate a set of print books and some marketing collateral as part of a program to offer to area book clubs.

Personal touches work best, so I go to many local libraries— we live in a library-rich area of New

England, and have hundreds of them within a 50-miles radius. They're more likely to stock books from people with local connections. This can include libraries in places you've lived and worked, went to school, or are in towns used in your book settings.

I offer my ebooks for free to libraries, because it costs me nothing to do so, and helps them. At one author event, I found out that many traditional publishing companies gouge libraries *more* for ebooks, and put restrictions on them. So I tell every librarian that I'll donate all my ebooks if they can get them into their system. I've done that successfully for a number of places. Most use the Overdrive system, but I haven't found a way to offer books for free from them, so we have to do a workaround.

But you don't get paid for that, you say. With almost every Indie author, the hard part is getting readers to *discover* your work, and there's no easier way than to have someone help get the word out. I've got a lot of offerings, and know my work is good. If someone discovers it through free means, still well and good. With most of them, they'll be back for more, and some will pay.

Other Listings

There are many places on the Internet where particular types of books are listed, and these are additional ways in which people can find your work. Some are genre sites, which lists genre authors, characters, and titles. Goodreads has a number of genre groups with listings, as well as Facebook. You'll have to hunt up some of these, and send notices of your work yourself, but they're worth running down. Always good to see your book listed in places where people might find it. All of it helps with search engines, too, getting your book tagged in numerous places.

Here's just a few useful ones, to give you an idea.

• https://www.bookseriesinorder.com/

• https://www.fictiondb.com/author/

• http://www.stopyourekillingme.com/

Genre organization sites, like MWA, SFWA, RWA, HWA, etc. also list member books. Add yours to the listings where appropriate. See if your higher learning institutions (your college) has listings from alumnae.

Dale T. Phillips

When you're ready for the Big Leagues, you can get your book into the Library of Congress. Check out the process and in a short time, you can have your work alongside the famous and revered. I was amazed that we Indie authors can make this happen. If anyone tweaks you as an Indie author of no consequence, you can slay them by saying your books are here.

How to Be a Successful Indie Writer

Appendices

Dale T. Phillips

Appendix A: Resources

Because links may disappear over time, use a search engine to find missing information.

When finding good resources, they'll often list more, so check out the places and books *they're* checking out. Start here:

The 100 Best Websites for Writers in 2020:

https://thewritelife.com/best-websites-for-writers-2020/

On Amazon, or other bookselling sites, enter a search term for the type of books you'd like, and check out the options. Because they list similar books in a category, you'll find lots of available sources for learning.

To be a successful writer takes years of sweat and solid effort, and studying the words of other writers. You need to have a love for the language, and a good comprehension of many concepts and themes of literature. So it's good to be familiar with the following:

- Roget's Thesaurus

Dale T. Phillips

- The Elements of Style, by Strunk and White

- Eats Shoots and Leaves, by Lynne Truss

- The works of Shakespeare

- The Odyssey

- Bulfinch's Mythology

- The Hero With a Thousand Faces, by Joseph Campbell

For Fiction, check out two classics of writer lives and struggles:

- Youngblood Hawke, by Herman Wouk (A fictionalized account of Thomas Wolfe- the older one)

- Martin Eden, By Jack London.

Success is not Linear:

https://www.wealest.com/articles/success-is-nonlinear

The Ten Thousand Hour Rule: From Malcom Gladwell in his book *Outliers: The Story of Success*. Quoted a lot, there's much more to it.

https://www.6seconds.org/2018/02/09/the-great-practice-myth-debunking-the-10000-hour-rule-and-what-you-actually-need-to-know-about-practice/#:~:text=What%20does%20it%20take%20to,more%20or%20less%20%E2%80%93%20completely%20false.

Seth Godin is a modern business guru with much to say about not needing permission to put out your idea to the world, along with creativity, business, and marketing tips.

https://www.sethgodin.com/

The Long Tail: Use this to understand that books will sell, though it may take years:

https://en.wikipedia.org/wiki/Long_tail

Blurbing/Tagline:

https://www.thefussylibrarian.com/newswire/for-authors/2019/12/13/how-to-write-a-book-blurb-crafting-an-attention-grabbing-summary-of-your-book

Story Submission markets:

Dale T. Phillips

- The Submission Grinder (free): https://thegrinder.diabolicalplots.com/

- Duotrope (pay): https://duotrope.com/

Formatting a Manuscript

https://www.shunn.net/format/classic/

Funding a project using Kickstarter:

https://kriswrites.com/2020/07/22/business-musings-the-kickstarted-game-changer-part-two/

Time Point Allotment

https://waitbutwhy.com/2016/10/100-blocks-day.html

How to Beat Procrastination

https://waitbutwhy.com/2013/11/how-to-beat-procrastination.html

Persistence and hard work:

I Can't make This Up: Life Lessons by Kevin Hart

Websites

Dean Wesley Smith posts a lot on business (and other things) for Indies.

https://www.deanwesleysmith.com/

His books are must-reads:

- Think Like A Publisher

- Killing the Sacred Cows of Publishing

- New World of Publishing

Blogs

Kristine Kathryn Rusch has a Thursday business posting that is a must for any Indie.

https://kriswrites.com/2020/07/01/business-musings-time-and-money-again/

These blogs for writers are interesting and often have useful information:

The Passive Voice: http://www.thepassivevoice.com/

Jane Friedman: https://www.janefriedman.com/blog/

Joanna Penn: https://www.thecreativepenn.com/

David Gaughran: https://davidgaughran.com/blog

Nathan Bransford: https://nathanbransford.com/blog

Susan Kay Quinn: http://susankayequinn.com/blog

Marketing/Promotion

All the marketing books of David Gaughran (also good YouTube videos)

https://davidgaughran.com/

The Secrets to Ebook Publishing Success– Mark Coker

20Booksto50K:
https://www.facebook.com/groups/20Booksto50k/

Some free Book listing sites (there are many more- just search for them):

- https://www.bookseriesinorder.com/

- https://www.fictiondb.com/author/

- http://www.stopyourekillingme.com/

Some websites want to charge you for online book promotion. Usually it's a variant of posting your book cover and link, and maybe a blurb, and sending it to subscribers, which

they claim will help sales. For some places, it's just a way for a site to make money from writers, but if you find one worth it, by all means, give it a go.

The Fussy Librarian:

https://www.thefussylibrarian.com/advertising/making -book-marketing-easier/

Book Gorilla:

https://www.bookgorilla.com/

BookBub (Tough to get into, and expensive, considered by many to be of value):

https://landing.bookbub.com/covers_ext_scrolling/?s ource=ba_us_bookbub_exact&utm_source=bing&utm _medium=cpc&utm_campaign=US- Brand%3A%20Bookbub&msclkid=44e10d81acc217c2 c367528849b43629

Dale T. Phillips

Ads

Vin Zandri's advice:

https://medium.com/@vincentzandri/how-its-possible-to-consistently-make-thousands-every-month-from-your-novels-with-minimal-97c10758b7a8

Publishing

The Newbie's Guide to Publishing– J.A. Konrath

The Self-Publishing Manual, Volume 1– Dan Poynter

How to Publish Your Novel– Ken Atchity

How to Publish a Book- Nathan Bransford

Write. Publish. Repeat. (The No-Luck-Required Guide to Self-Publishing Success) – Sean M. Platt and Johnny Truant

Business

The Copyright Handbook: What Every Writer Needs to Know

Rethinking the Writing Business: Kristine Kathryn Rusch

Taking the Mystery out of Business- Linda McHenry

How to Be a Successful Indie Writer

Indie Author Survival Guide– Susan Kaye Quinn

Pros and Cons- Jane Friedman

Thanks, But This Isn't For Us– Jessica Page Morrell

How to Be Your Own Literary Agent– Richard Curtis

Your Novel Proposal– Blythe Cameron and Marshall Cook

How to Become A Famous Writer Before You're Dead– Ariel Gore

Business Planning for Professional Publishers, Volume 5– Leah R Cutter

Tax Savvy for Small Businesses– Frederick W. Daily

Motivation/Writing Life

Motivate Your Writing– Stephen Kelner

The Productive Writer– Sage Cohen

Some Instructions on Writing and Life- Anne Lamott

The Writing Life- Annie Dillard

100 Things Every Writer Should Know– Scott Edelstein

Becoming a Writer– Dorothea Brande

Writer Tells All– Robert Massello

I'd Rather Be Writing– Marcia Golub

Honk If You're a Writer– Arthur Plotnik

Making a Literary Life– Carolyn See

Reading Like a Writer– Francine Prose

Writing Craft

The War of Art- Steven Pressfield

On Writing- Stephen King

The Writer's Journey- Christopher Vogler

The Forest for the Trees (Revised and Updated)- Betsy Lerner

An Editor's Advice to Writers- Betsy Lerner

Story Engineering- Larry Brooks

Naked, Drunk, and Writing- Adair Lara

Shed Your Inhibitions and Craft a Compelling Memoir or Personal Essay- Adair Lara

How to Write a Damn Good Novel- James N. Frey

Bird by Bird- Anne Lamott

How to Be a Successful Indie Writer

Modern Library Writer's Workshop– Stephen Koch

On Writing- Charles Bukowski

Wired for Story: The Writer's Guide to Using Brain Science to Hook Readers from the Very First Sentence- Lisa Cron

Writing Tools- Roy Peter Clark

On Writing Well- William Zinsser

Writing Down the Bones- Natalie Goldberg

Zen in the Art of Writing– Ray Bradbury

Story– Robert McKee

Stein on Writing, and How to Grow a Novel– Sol Stein

Lessons From a Lifetime of Writing: A Novelist Looks at His Craft- David Morrell

The Handbook of Short Story Writing, Volumes I and II, Frank Dickson and Sandra Smythe, Vol II edited by Jean Fredette

Steering the Craft– Ursula LeGuin

Writing the Novel, and Telling Lies for Fun and Profit– Lawrence Block

Creating Short Fiction– Damon Knight

Dale T. Phillips

On Writing– George V. Higgins

Reading & Writing– Robertson Davies

The Craft of Fiction– William Knott

The Complete Guide to Writing Fiction, edited by Barnaby Conrad

Learning to Write Fiction From the Masters– Barnaby Conrad

The Uses of Enchantment– Bruno Bettelhein

The Mystery Writer's Handbook, edited by Writer's Digest

Aspects of the Novel– E.M. Forster

The Writer's Craft– John Hersey

How To Write Your Novel– Margaret Chittenden

The Art of Creative Writing–Lajos Egri

This Year You Write Your Novel– Walter Mosley

The Craft of Writing– William Sloane

Write it Down– Henriette Klausen

Writing Mysteries, edited by Sue Grafton

Fiction First Aid– Raymond Ohstfeld

How to Be a Successful Indie Writer

The Plot Thickens, and The First Five Pages– Noah Lukeman

Writing the Modern Mystery– Barbara Norville

Writing the Blockbuster Novel– Albert Zuckerman

On Teaching and Writing Fiction– Wallace Stegner

How to Write a Damn Good Mystery– James Frey

The Writer's Idea Workshop– Jack Heffron

How to Write a Mystery– Larry Beinhart

Writer's Workshop in a Book, edited by Cheuse and Alvarez

Writing Fiction– Janet Burroway

The Elements of Mystery Fiction– William Tappley

Writing the Popular Novel– Loren Estleman

Novelist Boot Camp– Todd Stone

Fiction Writer's Workshop– Josip Nonakovich

How Fiction Works– James Woods

How to Write Mysteries– Shannon O'Cork

Talking About Detective Fiction– P.D. James

How to Write a Novel- Nathan Bransford

Dale T. Phillips

Other

Productivity for Creative People: How to get Creative Work Done in an "Always On" World – Mark McGuiness

The Daily Entrepreneur: 33 Success Habits for Small Business Owners, Freelancers, and Aspiring 9 to 5 Escape Artists – S.J. Scott and Rebecca Livermore

Manage Your Day to Day: Build Your Routine, Find Your Focus, and Sharpen Your Creative Mind – Jocelyn K. Glei & 99U Book Series

How to get things done with One Note – Dominic Wolfe

Completing The Writer's To-Do List. Magnolia Lane Press. Tonya D. Price

Getting Things Done: The Art of Stress-Free Productivity – David Allen

15 Secrets Successful People Know About Time Management – Kevin Druse

Appendix B: My Path

"It got too hard."

"It's *supposed* to be hard. If it wasn't hard, everyone would do it. The hard... is what makes it great."

—Geena Davis as Dorothy Hinson, and Tom Hanks as Jimmy Dugan, *A League of Their Own*

This section details my long, rocky, and twisted path to publication. You may find it useful, especially if you think your road is difficult, or you run into issues that force you to doubt or reconsider parts of your path to success. Remember, there are many paths to publication and success, and you should choose the one that's right for you. All this is here only as example and instruction.

I grew up in the pre-Internet era. The model of the path to successful publication was long-established and ironclad, allowing no deviation. You wrote a book, you queried an agent (by mail), and if a miracle occurred and you got an offer of representation, you did the Dance of Joy. The Big Step! Your agent then queried publishers. A few lucky writers would get an offer to publish their book, and sometimes it all worked, and the book came out. It was accepted as gospel that the publication industry would eventually find most (or all) really good and deserving books and publish them, if the writer kept at it long enough, so if a book didn't make it that far, well, it never really was good enough. Only the maniacally persistent and obsessive ever made it, usually after years of heartache and rejection.

So I walked that path, submitting and selling stories while I worked on novels.

Meanwhile, I worked to get a website and a blog created, and writer business cards printed, to start spreading the word about my writing aspirations. Laying the foundations for future success.

Stories

I began by keeping a log of story ideas and titles (now in the hundreds). Sometimes I would write a story from a prompt: a title, an idea, a scene, a character, an overheard bit of dialogue. With two fingers, I laboriously typed up tales, first on typewriters, then on word processors, with dot-matrix printouts.

Each year, I got a new copy of the expensive, thick, Writer's Market, and researched markets, agents, and publishers. I typed up each Self Addressed Stamped Envelope (SASE) and went to the post office to find out how much each story cost to mail. It wasn't cheap, and I didn't have any money to spare. Often you had to send a magazine a mailed query just to find out what they would buy. It was an expensive and time-consuming hobby.

Then I sold my first story, a good one, for decent money, except that the publisher's check bounced, and I got zinged by my bank for a bad check fee, which I never recovered. Ouch.

I sold another story, and another. Then there was a dry spell of years of nothing. The cost and *Pain In the Ass* (PITA) factor was too draining and time-consuming, few good markets remained, and after a while, I didn't submit anymore. Still dabbed away at the novel, still wrote, but wasn't pushing the stories to potential markets.

Submitting got easier in subsequent years. With ezines and online, there were more markets. There were online listings of those markets! You could now go to a magazine's website to see their guideline submissions! You could send a story by email, saving the cost of printing out the story, as well as sending the manuscript and return postage! You could get an answer back in weeks, instead of months in some cases!

An aspiring writer friend read my stories and persuaded me to start submitting again. When I did, it was a sea change, and more stories began to sell, which encouraged me to write more. Since then, I've made that a priority, always keeping unsold stories in constant rotating submission until they sell, or are included in a self-published collection. Magazine editors have no money to spare, and only buy the best they can find. They may get hundreds of submissions for an issue or an anthology, and can only publish a handful. So if you sell a story to them, it's usually good- **that's how you know you're progressing as a writer, when multiple, thin-pursed editors *pay* you**. So far, I've had over 70 stories published, and hope to have a few hundred more, if I get to live and produce for a few more years.

And then, following the advice of another Indie pub guru, Dean Wesley Smith (see Resources), I gathered stories into collections once I'd got the rights back, and put them up for sale on the Internet. They've sold hundreds and hundreds of copies, in print, as ebooks, and as audiobooks.

Old-School print publishers would seldom bother with story collections, even from best-selling novelists, because they wouldn't sell enough copies to be profitable. That path was dead, but Indie was *The Way* for story winning. I've found many new fans who started with my story collections.

Success- the hard way. Rather satisfying.

Novels

For years, I worked on an idea that I knew was a good story. (See *Case Studies*) As a first book, though, I had much to learn, and it was a long painful process trying to make the tale something good. Most people who start writing a book don't finish it, and out of those that do, many don't get it published.

Flawed though the book was, and completely non-commercial for Big Publishing, I began the query process to agents and a few publishers anyway. No bites, and some never bothered to even reply.

So I began writing my second novel, a mystery, and worked for a few years to make that commercial enough. Using what I'd learned writing the first book, I created a good, sellable story. Through a contact, I found an agent who read the manuscript, said that it was sellable, and agreed to represent me. He was out of the mainstream, but in those days, it was considered better to have any agent than none at all.

So months went by. Then more months. Then more. Welcome to traditional publishing, kiddies! We had an acquisitions editor at a smaller publishing house interested, but more and more months went by with no progress. I began to lose faith in the system, realizing I could die of old age before getting any books published. I parted with the agent (after a few years!), figuring I could do better elsewhere. I submitted the manuscript to a publisher who claimed interest, but who then never properly responded, costing me more months of waiting for nothing. I wondered (and despaired) how long it would take to get books actually published and into reader hands.

The world then changed, with the disruptive technology of ebooks, Amazon 24/7 distribution, and tools for profitable, smaller-scale publishing. I realized I could have control over my production, instead of eternally waiting for others. There was a lot of buzz about this self-publishing model. I was interested, but did not have the tools or experience to do it all on my own, though I was doing a lot of research. And learning fast. I teamed with a man who formed his own home-publishing business and put together an ebook about improving interviewing skills. It was an experiment to test the process and gauge the results. Funny thing, that little experiment is also in print and as an audiobook, and has sold hundreds of copies. That success convinced me to publish more non-fiction, like the book you're reading.

A friend wanted to start a small publishing business with another friend of his. They asked me if I'd like my novel to be the first one they published in print and as an ebook. Launching a new pub biz? *Hell, yeah*! I agreed, as long as I held the reins: I control content, price, cover, etc. No advance, as they had no money, but split the profits. So in 2011, my first novel was launched to the world. Success! I'd gone further than so many others. It was nice to get into bookstores and have the book available on their shelves, a lifetime goal. Some bookstores bought outright, some took consignment. I was on my way.

The second novel (second in the series) was published with them as well, not long after. By the time my third book was ready, they were publishing other writers, and were so busy they didn't have time to do mine as quickly as I wanted. So I published through the other small press, the one who had done my nonfiction book. Two different small presses, three novels, and a non-fiction help book.

Dale T. Phillips

It was success of a sort. Of course there were some hiccups. When you split profits with others, there's not much for you. Given the price point, I'd lose money with deep discounts, as bookstores take 40-50% of the cover price for themselves. There were a few mistakes along the way, and things still took longer than they should. By now, two years later, I'd learned enough about this self-publishing world, and could do everything they did faster, better, and with more profit. I'd tested the publishing process a few times with story collections, published through Amazon companies: CreateSpace and Kindle, and ACX/Audible for audiobooks.

Time to go from Small Press to full Independent. I formed my own company, easy enough in this state, requiring only a simple filing of paperwork, a bank account for the business, and a $40 fee for four years as a DBA- *Doing Business As* (which also can get you a *Tax Identification Number*- better than your Social Security number for tax purposes). With a company logo to imprint on the books, and a company website, I launched my own publishing house, and put out all works under that imprint. When the original small press closed, I got the rights back to my novels, as I did for the other company, and now have all my works under my personal umbrella.

How to Be a Successful Indie Writer

Now I publish on my own terms and time frame, and have total control over all aspects. I have not regretted it, and consider myself one of the happiest writers around (especially when so many others complain about various aspects of writing and publishing). Any mistakes are mine, and I only have to work with one jerk (me). I get to create and sell whenever and however I wish. And sales increase every year. To me, that's success.

Note: Before I got my first novel out, I attended a class reunion at my university, and they had built a new alumni library building, with one room holding the published books of all alums, especially the big display (shrine) to Stephen King. I vowed to have my books join those on the shelves, and made it happen just a few years later.

Dream achieved!

Dale T. Phillips

Appendix C: Case Studies

This section shows two case studies of my first two novels, to show the process of adding ideas while working through the building of a novel. It illustrates how an early novel transforms into a finished, publishable book. For these two, it was a complex process that took time. Later novels usually were finished much quicker, because having done it successfully a few times makes it more familiar, and you know what the process is like, and have a better understanding of how to get to the end product. With subsequent books in a series, you've built the world already, and so have a head start on characters and where the book will be going.

People sometimes ask how long it takes to write a novel- for me it's anywhere from six months to 35 years! It shows what obsession means to a writer. It's my journey, how I began writing novels and learned how to finish novels, and then spend the time to make them better, not giving up.

As always, *Your Mileage May Vary*.

Remember, though like bad judgment that leads to bad mistakes, which then leads to good judgment, writing a bad novel can help you learn how to write a good one. So don't worry if your first few attempts are a struggle to make something of value. It's part of the learning process.

Book One: Shadow of the Wendigo

I wrote the original Wendigo story back when I took writing courses from Stephen King at my college, many years ago. The image, the heart of the story, was so powerful, I knew I could expand the concept into an entire book, and this was the first attempt at a novel, my first book-length idea. It's based on an actual Native American legend, one widespread and ancient, common to a number of tribes over a vast area of North America. So much has been written about creating The Great American Novel, but as I love skewing things, I set to work on The Great Canadian Novel. It was a more natural setting for the tale.

Long after I wrote the early draft, I discovered the work of Joseph Campbell, and realized I'd written a perfect example of The Hero's Journey.

I treated the legend as different possibilities: was it a physical being come to life, a mass hallucination, a mental rationale for committing the ultimate taboo, or a clever insanity defense for a killer? It had a terrific opening, a great final scene. But there was that saggy middle, thousands of words of mostly two people talking, with about five actual pages of action. Not a good score for a suspense thriller. It was lacking, but I didn't know how to fix it. So into the drawer it went. And remember, this was in the Old Days, when this sucker was painstakingly typed out several times on a typewriter.

Insert years of life, pecking away at various stories. I began a second novel, a mystery, again expanded from a simple idea. While writing that, I realized I had a series on my hands. That book got to completion, and after a time, I started shopping around for a publisher. More years passed.

Dusting off the first novel. For the title, there are a number of books with *Wendigo* in their title. Although one cannot copyright a title, I wanted something that wouldn't get confusing on an Internet search. From time to time, I would work on *Shadow of the Wendigo*, moving from typewriter to the magic of word processing (phew!). I could fix the little things, even though the huge flaws seemed insurmountable. Along the way, I'd learned more about writing.

First, most of it was *telling*, not *showing*. You've likely run across the writing maxim *Show, don't Tell*. Stories can be interesting, but it's important how you present them. There was the basic three-act structure, so the skeleton was there. Another major problem was the lack of conflict. There was the main story, and the battle against the elements, but not enough else. Lackluster scene after scene. Yawn. Bit by bit, I raised the stakes in different scenes. For example, the protagonist and his wife were too domestically happy when they're introduced as a couple. They needed a big problem, and they got one. Spiced up every interaction.

While having The Hero and The Mentor do a lot of talking was classical story-telling, they also got along too well. Well, hell, that's no fun, so The Mentor became a lot crankier. When I added a comic foil, a sidekick for some back-and-forth interactions, I realized he was the mythological Fool, fitting in nicely. He brought a new dimension to many scenes, saying things that would be wrong coming from the mouths of other characters. Apart from a necessary touch of lightness at needed points, he also added tension and conflict to other scenes.

Okay, so we had good bits and pieces, and some flashes of what could be. But still missing important things. While studying more work on writing, I came across an explanation of why the hero needs a powerful antagonist, to make an elemental battle. Within the book, the "supernatural" element was an obstacle to the hero, as was the harsh environment itself, but it wasn't enough. An antagonist was needed.

In a writing critique group I was in, we gave feedback to another writer on his suspense novel, and suggested he turn his clichéd assassin into a female, to spark the level from humdrum to interesting. He didn't want to do the work of rewriting, but the idea stuck with me. How would a powerful female antagonist manifest in my novel? At an author show, one author had an interesting job title. So two things came together in the form of a woman *cryptozoologist*, and she would be resourceful, rich, and driven, and be quite the obstacle for the Hero, with competing goals. Later I realized she fulfilled the classical mythological role of Coyote, The Trickster. Wow. When this stuff comes together, it can do so with a vengeance. She didn't just *enter* the book, she blew the doors off. After much rewriting, she was ensconced as a major character, who drives much of the action.

Originally, I'd had a prologue, and via feedback, had been convinced to shed it. There were four good chapters to start the book, but that left a problem, as we didn't meet the Hero until chapter five. A bit late, with no setup. Not good, didn't want readers saying *who's this guy?* But he was in a different place, and I didn't want a back-and-forth jump cuts used by so many thriller writers. Solution: a short, short prologue to introduce the main character and set the unsettled mood with a deep foreboding. Followed by the action of the four chapters, it fit nicely.

So over time it developed into something worthwhile. The more I saw, the more it began to mesh. The ingredients began to gel in a cohesive fashion, becoming a smooth ride with conflict enough to move the story along. The things I'd learned to do as a writer were tools to help me understand and incorporate the structure and technique of long-form storytelling.

I had to write and publish three other novels before this one was published, and it was my first standalone, a non-series book, published in 2014. And readers loved it. People asked for a sequel, even though it was always meant as a standalone. A great compliment to the characters, that readers wanted to see more of them.

One listener to the audio book was a mailman, and stopped his route to text me how much he was loving the story. But he had to alter his route to get to a WiFi spot. Other told me at length how they responded to the characters. One huge, burly guy told me it had given him the first nightmare he'd had in years, and another reviewer said something similar. Top marks for a book with horror elements!

The lesson is, if a novel isn't working and you don't know how to fix it, it's okay to set it aside and work on other books that will sell. Keep writing, keep learning, keep moving forward. But you don't have to abandon it for good, unless the story is just no good. If something matters enough so that you've started, you may want to give it another shot after you've improved your skills.

Book Two: A Memory of Grief

When *Shadow of the Wendigo* went into the trunk, I needed a new idea for the next novel, and wanted to do better with this one, make it good enough to attract an agent (back when that was my path) and one of the bigger publishers. So it would need to be in a sellable genre, and sage writing advice is to write the kind of book you'd like to read, so I set out to do just that.

Raymond Chandler said that mystery and detective stories sell better over time than other books, and luckily, I loved mysteries, detective, and Private Investigator novels, from Dashiell Hammett to

Chandler, to Mickey Spillane, up through to Robert B. Parker and more. But one of my all-time favorite writers is John D. MacDonald, and his much-beloved Travis McGee series is just the best ever. McGee was a knockabout Florida eccentric who had no regular job, lived on a houseboat, and helped people who'd lost something valuable recover part of that, taking half the value for his trouble and expenses. He was a pirate with a conscience, and loved life, though living out of the mainstream.

My character would have some similarities, but be different enough so that he would stand on his own. He'd be an amateur investigator, like Travis, though mine accidentally gets into helping people in trouble. When the first book begins, he hears of the death of his best friend, a supposed suicide, and he travels to Maine to find out the truth. Complications ensue.

That was the simplicity of the start- a man looks into the death of a friend. For the setting, I chose my much-loved Portland, Maine, where I lived for a time. This would take the book out from the familiar detective novels set in gritty big cities like New York, Chicago, and L.A., where the place is as much character as anybody in the novel. Maine is quite different, and the differences would matter.

How to Be a Successful Indie Writer

My character wouldn't have the connections or advantages that most crime investigators have- he'd be an outsider, a stranger in a strange land. He wouldn't have the helpers, especially the homicidal sidekick seen in so many books of this type- they're interesting characters, but too *deus ex machina* for my taste, since they always show up when needed, and help dispatch the bad guys without any pause or regret or aftereffects. Too easy.

My protagonist would be out of the mainstream, with particular skills that would help him in his quest. I did away with the usual ex-military or ex-cop characters, preferring something less ordinary. But who would have acquaintance with violence, and crime, and be willing to take on dangerous tasks? Perhaps someone who'd been in jail, had some darkness in his background. An interesting character.

A common trope of detective novels is where the protagonist whips out a gun, and gets out of danger by winning every shootout. I wanted something different, something not so easy. How about a main character who didn't like guns? He'd have to rely on wits and physical skills. Okay, so what kind of person would that be? Someone who suffered a terrible tragedy when

273

younger, that makes him hate guns. Ah, backstory and depth.

But if he got involved close-up with dangerous people, he'd need something. I've got an extensive background in various types of Martial Arts, so I made him a fighter, quite used to physical violence. It helped his backstory, showing how he works hard to control himself, because his anger, guilt, and shame drove him into his alternate lifestyle and pursuit of physical violence.

His way of living got him involved with criminals, and he got in trouble with law enforcement, and spent time in jail for not being able to control himself. Now he lives in the shadows, with few commitments, and works as a bouncer and bodyguard. But he has learned how to read people, know when they're lying, and when they're about to erupt into violence.

We needed a name for this character, one that sounds like a man of action. Zack Taylor took shape, named for President Zachary Taylor, an obscure figure to most, but with more meaning and punch than say, Bob Jones.

Note: *Another writer friend chose the name **Jack Taylor** for his thriller novel character, completely without knowledge of mine. Synchronicity.*

Now Zack's situation would have many disadvantages, and his way of acting would be uncontrolled, a bull in a china shop. This would make things fun, because it makes for constant conflict, and the reader would never know when he would lose control and slip over the edge. His method of investigation is to start questioning people involved in the crime, and see their reactions. When people start lying, he tries to figure out why, and does a lot of following and stakeouts, eventually turning up secrets. He makes mistakes, and innocent people get hurt, which only adds to his guilt and anger. He's also a pirate, and isn't averse to scooping up loose piles of illicit loot. The plot grew as Zack had interactions with others, and even developed a romantic interest while investigating. Bit by bit, the novel took shape, and I realized that I'd created a world that needed to live beyond just this novel, into a series of adventures.

I found another way to make the book more meaningful. The title came from the pre-Biblical story *The Epic of Gilgamesh*, the oldest tale we have. It tells of a powerful king whose companion was killed, and the king loses his mind with grief, going completely off the rails, a sort of echo of what happens to Zack (and more beyond that). I liked the title concept so much I used literary references in subsequent series titles, using quotes from Emily Dickinson to Nathaniel Hawthorne, which all reflected what was happening in the book and adding to the theme.

I wrote the first chapter, as a prologue, no less, and took it to my writing critique group, who ripped it apart. All agreed it wasn't a good start, which shocked me. Rather than argue, I did what a writer should do: study the comments and check for validity. If a book doesn't resonate with a group, maybe they've got a point.

So I rewrote the chapter and tried again. Nope, not there yet. I kept at it, learning more each time. Did it more than a few times. Scratch the prologue, jump right into the story. I put in the work, and eventually had a great first chapter which set the scene and plot for the book, introduced the main character, and gave enough information to make the reader want to move on.

In books after that, the opening of each book came much easier. I'd learned where and how to start the story, which many writing instructors say is the most important thing. Without a good opening, the reader may not care to go on. Start well, and go from there.

Appendix D: Feedback

We all can learn from constructive feedback. Your comments would be helpful in making future versions of this book more useful to writers.

- Was this book helpful?

- Was anything unclear?

- Was anything in error or misleading?

- What should be added?

As a way of saying thank you for reading this and offering your feedback on the content, I'd like to offer you a free ebook of your choice from my works. Contact me and let me know which one you'd like, and I'll send download instructions.

Dale T. Phillips

Acknowledgments

As with many large projects, a number of people were involved in the creation and distribution of this book. And many more were influences, by their words and deeds. Thanks to all who helped by their examples and advice.

Special thanks go out to Connie Johnson Hambley, Ursula Wong, and Claudia Decker for their attention to detail in helping make the manuscript better.

Dedication

To all the hard-working writers who put in the effort to be successful.

Dale T. Phillips

About the Author

Dale T. Phillips has combined years of study into this work. He studied writing with Stephen King, and has published novels, over 70 short stories, collections, as well as poetry, articles, and non-fiction. He has appeared on stage, television, and in an independent feature film. He has also appeared on *Jeopardy*, losing in a spectacular fashion. He co-wrote and acted in a short political satire film. He has traveled to all 50 states, Mexico, Canada, and through Europe.

Connect Online:
Website: http://www.daletphillips.com
Blog: http://daletphillips.blogspot.com/
Facebook:
https://www.facebook.com/DaleTPhillips/
Twitter: DalePhillips2

Try these other works by Dale T. Phillips

Shadow of the Wendigo (Supernatural Thriller)
Neptune City (Mystery)

The Zack Taylor Mystery Series
A Darkened Room
A Sharp Medicine
A Certain Slant of Light
A Shadow on the Wall
A Fall From Grace
A Memory of Grief

Story Collections
The Big Book of Genre Stories (Different Genres)
Halls of Horror (Horror)
Deadly Encounters (3 Zack Taylor Mystery/Crime Tales)
The Return of Fear (Scary Stories)
Five Fingers of Fear (Scary Stories)
Jumble Sale (Different Genres)
Crooked Paths (Mystery/Crime)

Dale T. Phillips

More Crooked Paths (Mystery/Crime)
The Last Crooked Paths (Mystery/Crime)
Fables and Fantasies (Fantasy)
More Fables and Fantasies (Fantasy)
Strange Tales (Magic Realism, Paranormal)
Apocalypse Tango (End of the World)

Non-fiction Career Help
How to be a Successful Indie Writer
How to Improve Your Interviewing Skills

With Other Authors
Rogue Wave: Best New England Crime Stories 2015
Red Dawn: Best New England Crime Stories 2016
Windward: Best New England Crime Stories 2017

Sign up for my newsletter to get special offers
http://www.daletphillips.com